THE
SECRET
LIVES
OF THE NAZIS

THE SECRET LIVES OF THE NAZIS

The Hidden History of the Third Reich

PAUL ROLAND

SIRIUS

SIRIUS

This edition published in 2017 by Sirius Publishing, a division of
Arcturus Publishing Limited,
26/27 Bickels Yard, 151–153 Bermondsey Street,
London SE1 3HA

ISBN: 978-1-78428-896-9
AD005415UK

Printed in Singapore

Contents

Introduction

Adolf Hitler and the Nazi leaders conspired to commit some of the most heinous crimes in history, for which the surviving members were indicted at Nuremberg in 1946. However, both the defendants and those in the regime who evaded justice perpetrated countless acts of murder, torture, theft, false imprisonment, abduction and intimidation for which they were never prosecuted.

While they were demanding that the German people make sacrifices in order to finance a war which few in Hitler's inner circle believed they could win, they themselves were living a life of privilege and power, acquiring priceless private art collections looted from the treasure houses of Europe and amassing vast personal fortunes stolen from the conquered countries and their countless victims.

Goering, Goebbels, von Ribbentrop and other prominent Nazis justified the seizure of more than £500 million ($650m) worth of gold bullion from banks in occupied Europe by citing International Law, which entitled the victors to claim the assets of their defeated enemies. But as *The Secret Lives of the Nazis* reveals, the scale of the looting and property theft fulfilled a secret agenda. The systematic theft of each nation's assets and those of selected individuals was part of a master plan to demoralize their defeated enemies and fund Germany's ambitions for world domination. Even the genocide of the Jews may not have been implemented solely on racial grounds, but also to rob a race of its wealth.

The Secret Lives of the Nazis uncovers the criminal nature of this brutal and corrupt regime and its murderous private feuds, as the leadership vied with each other for the Führer's favours and fought to assert their authority in an administration that was as unstable and self-destructive as its leader.

Rogues' Gallery

Joseph Goebbels, the cynical and pathologically self-absorbed Nazi spin doctor, exploited his position as Propaganda Minister to carry on a series of clandestine affairs with beautiful movie starlets and to furnish his offices and private apartments with priceless rugs, antiques and artwork paid for out of Reich Ministry funds.

Despite the image he liked to project of himself as Hitler's most trusted aide, Goebbels was excluded from all important policy decisions and was deeply troubled by his wife's evident infatuation with Hitler. Even after their marriage, Goebbels suffered sleepless nights tormented by the thought that his wife might only have married him to be closer to Hitler.

Hitler in turn cynically manipulated his disciple's slavish loyalty by flattering the man who was called 'the poison dwarf' by his enemies. Goebbels sought to compensate for his physical deformity by creating an overpowering personality and indulging his insatiable sexual appetite, bedding countless women whose conquest he recorded in his voluminous diaries. Though a rabid anti-Semite, he carried on a long affair with a Jewish actress and obsessively logged the number of times he slept with her. He was loathed by the other Nazi leaders and hated them in return, venting his rage against his political rivals, particularly Goering, whom he described as 'a lump of frozen shit'.

Alfred Rosenberg, the self-styled Nazi 'philosopher' who originated the myth of the Aryan Master Race, was despised by both Goering and Goebbels for his sycophantic fawning to Hitler and for his relentless whining that he had been excluded from the Führer's inner circle. Rosenberg was yet another member of the administration who ignored his own dictates when it suited him. A virulent anti-Semite, he made no secret of keeping a Jewish mistress. He was, however, tortured by the fact that no one in the Nazi leadership took him or his fanciful theories seriously. Even Hitler privately dismissed his anti-Semitic tracts as 'illogical rubbish'.

Martin Bormann, Hitler's private secretary, was universally despised by the Nazi elite for barring their access to the Führer. A ruthless intriguer, he kept secret files on the private indiscretions committed by his rivals and those he could coerce into acting as informants. Though outwardly a committed family man, he convinced his wife to share their home with his mistress and allow him to father more children with her. Instrumental in prosecuting the clergy on trumped-up charges of corruption and sexual abuse in order to discredit the Church and replace Christianity with Nazi ideology, he was also a chief instigator of 'the Final Solution', which saw the systematic murder of Jews and the theft of their personal wealth.

Hans Frank, the sadistic governor general of Poland, lived like a prince in an opulent palace while presiding over a slave-state. He objected to execution without trial on the grounds that it undermined the Nazi judicial system, and yet he personally ordered the herding of Jews into ghettos and their subsequent extermination.

Heinrich Himmler used his influence as head of the SS and the Gestapo to oversee the theft of billions of pounds' worth of assets from both Jews and non-Jews alike and the systematic asset stripping of financial institutions in Germany and the occupied countries. The former poultry farmer became the most feared man in the Third Reich, with the power of life and death over millions both inside Germany and in the occupied territories, where his SS 'elite' murdered with impunity.

Though he professed to be a happily married man and a faithful husband, he carried on a lengthy extramarital affair with a secretary who bore him two children. And despite being described by his subordinates as something of a prude, he took an abnormally active interest in the private lives of his men, which bordered on the voyeuristic, as well as in the sinister *Lebensborn* (Fount of Life) breeding programme in which SS men were allocated a pre-selected mate with whom to propagate the Aryan 'Master Race'. When the project failed to produce enough progeny, Himmler ordered the forced abduction of tens of thousands of suitably Aryan-looking children from the Eastern occupied territories.

The Reichsführer SS also presided over the forced sterilization programme which saw 320,000 healthy German women, some as young as 15, subjected to operations because they were judged to be not sufficiently 'pure' to bear children for the Reich. Hundreds died from the botched operations and from complications and infections, while many more were psychologically damaged from being officially declared either 'unfit to marry' or 'mentally feeble'.

Reinhard Heydrich, Himmler's second-in-command, considered himself an intelligent and cultured man. He played the violin and confessed that he found executions 'horrifying', though the gassing of Jews was strangely 'calming'. A serial womanizer, he was instrumental in baiting the honey trap known as Salon Kitty, a Berlin brothel wired with surveillance devices to eavesdrop on the intimate confessions and pillow talk of high-ranking German army officers and foreign diplomats. He also plotted the murder of Sturmabteilung (SA) leaders and other rivals on the 'Night of the Long Knives' in June 1934, which left the SS as the dominant instrument of terror in the Nazi state.

Hermann Goering, the corpulent commander-in-chief of the Luftwaffe, had no illusions regarding the danger posed by the SA, whose death warrant he signed on 30 June 1934, though his barely repressed hatred of its leader Ernst Röhm and his homosexual lieutenants might be a case of Caliban's revulsion on seeing his own reflection.

'The SA was nothing but a mob of gangsters and perverts!' roared the debauched Reichsmarschall, who had a penchant for wearing make-up, flaunting his jewellery and dressing like a 'perfumed Nero'.

Goering, a former First World War fighter ace and morphine addict, acquired a vast private collection of priceless art by deceit, fraud, theft and intimidation. He routinely resorted to blackmail, bribes and the bugging of his rivals' phones to keep tabs on their plots to oust him.

Together these men conspired to commit the most cynical and audacious crimes of the 20th century, in which gold bullion, business assets, priceless art and personal property were only part of the plunder stolen to order. Antiques, rare manuscripts and books, religious artefacts, gems, statues, tapestries, porcelain and even tens of thousands of bottles of vintage wine were just part of a hoard which in 1945 was estimated as amounting to one-fifth of the world's art treasures, much of which remains unaccounted for more than 70 years later.

Fated to Fail

The criminal nature of the Nazi regime with its unquestioning obedience and inflexible adherence to the Führer principle fatally undermined its effectiveness. Hitler's desire to establish a quasi-religious cult-cum-feudal society based on an unstable hierarchy with a messianic figure at its head (and a false prophet at that), served by fawning acolytes, was fated to fail. This continual struggle for supremacy and authority over one another was further compounded by Hitler's insistence that his subordinates must deal with the confusion he had created and that he should not be troubled with the details. As a result, no one took the initiative to address critical conflicts of interest, most of them stemming from the fact that every state department was duplicating the tasks allocated to its equivalent Party office.

Hitler did not possess the ability to govern, only to motivate his minions to seek ways of pleasing him. They saw him as a visionary when he was little more than an idle dreamer. He had been elevated by a quirk of fate to govern a nation he was not capable or competent to lead anywhere but to the abyss.

Had the German people known the truth about the men they entrusted with their future, history might have taken a very different turn.

Chapter One

SEX, DRUGS AND DOUBLE STANDARDS

'What luck for the rulers that men do not think.'

Adolf Hitler

Only in Nazi Germany could a government official excite himself over the discovery that his Führer's cook was one thirty-second Jewish and consider the matter sufficiently significant to mark it 'Top Secret', as Himmler's lieutenant Adolf Eichmann did.

Only in Nazi Germany could two functionaries become bitter enemies because one favoured a specific method of execution over another, as did Rudolf Hoess and Christian Wirth, rival death camp commandants whose quarrel had nothing to do with which lethal gas (carbon monoxide or Zyklon B) was the more humane, but which was the more efficient method of murder.

Only in Hitler's nightmare state could such amoral nonentities acquire the power of life and death over their fellow human beings, whom their psychotic leader had classified as *Untermenschen* (subhumans) and had deemed 'unworthy of life'.

Nazi Germany was Hitler's psychosis made manifest, a Kafkaesque world of oppressive surveillance and suspicion, of amoral laws enforced by terror, torture and intimidation: one in which children were encouraged to inform on their parents, where the law was used to prosecute the innocent and where no dissenter dared express their thoughts for fear of being dragged off to a concentration camp in the middle of the night without trial, under the criminal decree known as 'Night and Fog'. But then Nazi Germany was a gangster state run by criminals, psychopaths, sadists and self-serving petty bureaucrats.

It was the age of gangsterism, with criminals profiting from an unpopular law (Prohibition) in America and fascist governments exploiting political instability and financial insecurity in Europe, while Stalin presided over a reign of terror in the name of communism in Soviet Russia.

Night of the Long Knives

It was not mere competition for the Führer's favours that fuelled the Nazi leaders' enmity, but a vicious personal rivalry, one that would mean death for one or more members of Hitler's inner circle if the opportunity presented itself. For that reason, Propaganda Minister Joseph Goebbels had rushed to Bad Wiessee in Upper Bavaria to be with Hitler on the Night of the Long Knives (the Röhm putsch) on 30 June 1934, rather than remain in Berlin where he feared he might be added to the list of victims being drawn up by Goering and Himmler.

It was only after he had satisfied himself that he could still count on Hitler's protection that Goebbels returned to the capital to coordinate the propaganda campaign that attempted to justify the murder of the SA leadership and dozens of political rivals as a necessary act of 'self-defence' by the state.

For some months Röhm had been demanding that his Brownshirts should be officially recognized as an autonomous militia and incorporated into the regular army. This was something Hitler could not permit for it would antagonize the army High Command who would then have a legitimate reason to stage their own coup. And so the SA was falsely accused of plotting to overthrow the National Socialist government barely a year after it had seized power. Hitler had prevaricated for some time, reluctant as ever to make a decision when one was needed, and only gave the order when presented with fake documents purportedly written by Röhm, ordering the assassination of his Führer as the first act in the coup.

In his broadcast and subsequent press conference Goebbels added that many of those involved in the alleged coup were 'asocial' or 'diseased elements', by which he meant homosexuals, for whom the serial seducer had a particular aversion. By alluding to this 'cancerous element' within the Party, Goebbels gave the impression that the regime would act as defender of the moral health of the nation, an assurance which he and the other Nazi leaders were ill-qualified to give.

The Hitler Enigma

'Does it not constitute a danger to the Nazi movement if it can be said that Nazi leaders are chosen for sexual reasons?'

Heinrich Himmler

Conflicted Personality

Hitler and his acolytes promoted National Socialism as a radical and popular political movement, but it differed in one very significant aspect from the totalitarian regimes that took root in Italy under Mussolini and in Spain under Franco. Nazi Germany was – in essence – the manifestation of a personality cult whose most ardent followers were in thrall to a malignant narcissist who demanded devotion or death. He in turn served their need for a redeemer after the humiliating defeat of the 1914–18 war and the abdication of the Kaiser.

They revered him as the saviour of Germany and spoke of him in quasi-religious terms.

'I looked into his eyes and he looked into mine,' recalled an anonymous admirer, 'and I was left with only one wish – to be at home and alone with the great overwhelming experience.'

Hitler used the National Socialist German Workers' Party (NSDAP) as a platform for his own ends, to enable him to seize power and exercise control over every aspect of his subjects' lives, from the ideological indoctrination of children to the extermination of the mentally and physically disabled who were deemed 'unworthy of life'. Like all tyrants and dictators, Hitler was a paranoiac who having taken power by subterfuge and secured it by force, imposed his will by terror and intimidation.

> **HITLER USED THE NATIONAL SOCIALIST GERMAN WORKERS' PARTY (NSDAP) AS A PLATFORM FOR HIS OWN ENDS, TO ENABLE HIM TO SEIZE POWER**

The Party slogan '*Ein Volk, ein Reich, ein Führer*' ('One people, one nation, one leader') was intended to convey a unity of purpose under one benevolent father figure, but it more accurately expressed Hitler's abnormal identification with a nation that he would ultimately abandon to its fate after it had failed him and whose destruction he would demand in order to punish it for having betrayed him.

Hitler was a violently conflicted personality who believed that he was always right, that no opinion other than his own was worth hearing, and who demanded absolute, unquestioning obedience. This psychosis and volatility was rooted in his early life and may have derived partly from his aberrant sexuality.

Early Life

Fascism has long been suspected of having a particularly strong appeal for the disaffected and discontented, who harbour a burning desire to be recognized and have their extremist opinions and distorted values validated by like-minded individuals.

The abuse Hitler suffered at the hands of his violent, domineering father and his over-identification with his indulgent and doting mother may have contributed to his conflicted personality, but whether it was nature or nurture that formed his character, Hitler grew up hating the world.

He had a particular loathing for his teachers, who described him as 'argumentative, autocratic, self-opinionated', lacking in self-control and bad-tempered. And he, in turn, dismissed them as 'erudite apes', 'effete' and 'mentally deranged', which says more about his need to justify his lack of academic qualifications and eventual expulsion than it does about those he disparaged. During his five years at *Realschule* (secondary or high school), he was prohibited from progressing to the next class on two occasions and had to repeat the entire year.

The hateful child grew into a belligerent young man who despised those who were cleverer and more accomplished than he – he discarded his one and only friend, August Kubizek, when the young pianist was accepted into a conservatoire shortly after Hitler had been rejected by the Academy of Fine Arts in Vienna. Unable to accept the possibility that he did not possess sufficient talent, he blamed the admissions committee which, he subsequently discovered, included four Jews. He later claimed to have written to the Director of the Academy, threatening that 'the Jews will pay!'

As he prowled the streets of the Austrian capital, bemoaning his fate and looking for someone to blame for it, he claimed to have been transfixed by the appearance of an Orthodox Jew in a long black coat and wearing the traditional sidelocks. His self-loathing was turned on a convenient scapegoat and in that moment Hitler realized that he had found an outlet for his bitterness and innate hostility.

'Wherever I went,' he later wrote, 'I began to see Jews and the more I saw, the more sharply they became distinguished in my eyes from the rest of humanity . . . I began to hate them . . . I had ceased to be a weak-kneed cosmopolitan and became an anti-Semite.'

Hitler began reading the anti-Semitic literature that was on sale openly in Vienna at the time; pamphlets and periodicals such as *Ostara*, which mixed pseudo-*völkisch* 'mysticism' with extreme nationalism and anti-Semitism. These hysterical texts with their crude pornographic cartoons reinforced his prejudices and gratified his sadistic sexual fantasies.

He would later romanticize his lonely years as an itinerant artist in Vienna because it served the myth that he had risen from obscurity to greatness by the blessing of Providence, the same invisible hand of fate that enabled him to survive several assassination attempts and which instilled in him a sense of destiny. But the years in Vienna may not have been as hard as Hitler later claimed. His total income inherited from his late parents, an aunt's bequest and an orphan's pension that he obtained by falsely claiming to be an art student amounted to 100 kronen a month (roughly the equivalent of £650/$830 in 2016), which he supplemented by begging.

The tramps with whom he lived for a time in a charity ward at Meidling resented the fact that he wouldn't take the labouring jobs that they were prepared to accept, although he later falsely claimed to have worked on a building site. His claim to have become an anti-Semite on seeing an Orthodox Jew is also suspect as he was known to have befriended a Hungarian Jew named Neuman in the Meidling hostel and to have accepted a gift of a frock coat from him.

Here among the flea-ridden dosshouses and charity hostels of Vienna, Hitler festered in envy and resentment at the world that had rejected him and fermented his nihilist philosophy, which held that life was a 'brutal struggle' (*Mein Kampf*), a creed engendered by what Joachim Fest called 'the hate and impotence of the outcast'. In projecting his own compulsion for revenge on to a convenient scapegoat and attributing his paranoia to an imaginary cabal of conspirators, Hitler attempted to assuage the turmoil within his own troubled psyche.

His only friend Kubizek observed: 'He saw everywhere only obstacles and hostility. He was always up against something and at odds with the world . . . I never saw him take anything lightly.'

Nothing Hitler subsequently said regarding his early life was to be taken on trust. He even lied about welcoming the declaration of war in 1914 as the hour of his 'deliverance', for in fact he had evaded compulsory military service. When he was finally traced and called to account he wrote a long, emotional letter to the Linz Municipal Council pleading for leniency, which betrayed an uncommonly poor command of the German language.

It has since been revealed that the famous photograph purporting to show the 25-year-old Hitler cheering the declaration of war as he stood in the crowd at Munich's Odeonsplatz on 2 August is most likely a fake. He doesn't appear on any other photograph of the crowd taken on that day or in the newsreel footage.

The photo first appeared in the German *Illustrated Observer* in 1932 on the very day that Hitler declared himself a candidate for the presidency. Not once in the 12 years since joining the NSDAP had he mentioned being present on that historic day, which he surely would have done as he could have made considerable political capital from it. The original caption arouses suspicion by describing Hitler as 'the German patriot' and conveniently providing the perfect photographic proof. Hitler, it would seem, was rewriting his own history in the certainty that no one at the time would look too closely or ask too many questions.

It is likely that the murders of Ernst Röhm and other SA leaders may have been prompted by something more sinister than political infighting – the necessity to silence those who knew the secrets of Hitler's youth.

Hitler was so fearful of anyone finding out about his family origins that one of the first orders he issued after the annexation of Austria in 1938 was for the obliteration of the village of Dollersheim, his father's birthplace and the site of his grandmother's grave.

At the time he was quoted as saying: 'These people

[journalists] must never find out who I am. They mustn't know where I come from or my family background.'

Hitler and Men

Samuel Igra, author of *Germany's National Vice*, claimed that Hitler had been a male prostitute in Vienna between 1907 and 1912, and that he lived by those means again in Munich between 1912 and 1914, when the Great War offered him a reprieve. It has been argued that Igra was a Jewish writer who would have had a reason to vilify Hitler by making accusations of that nature, but historian Desmond Seward had no hidden agenda when he wrote in *Napoleon and Hitler* that Hitler was listed as a homosexual in Viennese police records.

'EVEN TODAY, HITLER DERIVES SEXUAL PLEASURE FROM LOOKING AT MEN'S BODIES AND ASSOCIATING WITH HOMOSEXUALS'

The American psychologist Walter Langer was commissioned by the OSS (a forerunner of the CIA) to compile a psychological profile of the dictator in 1943, for which he and his team interviewed hundreds of former associates of the regime and disaffected émigrés. From them, Langer derived the allegation that Hitler 'chose to live in a Vienna flophouse known to be inhabited by many homosexuals'.

'Even today, Hitler derives sexual pleasure from looking at men's bodies and associating with homosexuals.'

Such rumours do not, of course, constitute evidence, but then there is the fact of Hitler's close association with the openly gay Röhm and the question of his odd relationship with Rudolf Hess. Röhm and Hess were the only two men whom Hitler habitually addressed with the intimate and affectionate term '*du*'.

After his release from Landsberg prison Hitler fretted over the fact that Hess would not be released for some time, in terms that were inappropriate when one man was speaking of another. '*Ach mein Rudy, mein Hesserl*,' Hitler was reported as saying, using Austrian diminutives that were more commonly used in referring to children or loved ones.

One of Hitler's valets had his suspicions about the real nature of Hitler's relationship with Hess, who was allegedly known as 'Fräulein Anna' among the Munich transsexuals. The servant noted how excited Hitler would get whenever he created an architectural drawing that delighted him or received a particularly valuable gift. He would run to Hess to show him as a child runs to its mother. One of these was a handwritten love letter that King Ludwig II of Bavaria, Wagner's patron, had written to a manservant.

There was only one witness to Hitler's alleged homosexuality and that was Hans Mend, a dispatch rider who had served in the same regiment as Hitler and claimed to have seen him in a compromising situation with another man.

If Hitler had been a practising homosexual as has been alleged, or if, as seems more likely, he was either a latent homosexual or asexual, he had to be seen to take a stand against it whenever accusations were levelled at the SA or at the effeminate Schirach.

Hitler once 'lectured' Rudolf Diels, the founder of the Gestapo, on the role of homosexuality in history, who later recalled what the Führer had told him.

'It had destroyed ancient Greece, he said. Once rife, it extended its contagious effects like an ineluctable law of nature to the best and most manly of characters, eliminating from the reproductive process precisely those men on whose offspring a nation depended. The immediate result of the vice was, however, that unnatural passion swiftly became dominant in public affairs if it were allowed to spread unchecked.'

The National Socialists were characteristically two-faced when it came to the issue of homosexuality. They tolerated it when it concerned their own, but in public they condemned it as 'deviant' behaviour as is shown by their policy edict issued on 14 May 1928:

'It is not necessary that you and I live, but it is necessary that the German people live. And it can live if it can fight, for life means fighting. And it can only fight if it maintains its masculinity. It can only maintain its masculinity if it exercises discipline, especially in matters of love. Free love and deviance are undisciplined. Therefore, we reject you, as we reject anything which hurts our people. Anyone who even thinks of homosexual love is our enemy.'

However, in private, the Party was sharply divided between those who spoke openly against it – Himmler being one of the most vociferous – and those like Hitler who grudgingly tolerated it, so long as it didn't cause a scandal that could damage the Party's electoral chances.

Hitler and Röhm

The one issue that both factions could agree upon was the threat posed to the Party by the SA, the unruly paramilitary unit commanded by the brutal hot-headed thug Ernst Röhm, who made no attempt to hide his homosexual activities or those of his men. Many of them were recruited and promoted because they had found favour with Röhm and his senior officers, namely Karl Ernst the SA commander in Berlin and Edmund Heines, who was Röhm's deputy. Heines was said to have earned his promotion after scouting Munich for handsome new recruits.

In *The Nazi Extermination of Homosexuals*, historian Frank Rector wrote that Hitler was frequently referred to as '*Schoen Adolf*' (handsome Adolf) and that Ernst Röhm's affluent gay friends were early supporters of the NSDAP – the implication being that they were attracted primarily by the culture of homosexuality prevalent in the SA rather than its political ambitions.

Röhm saw no reason for discretion and made no effort to keep reports of his frequent orgies and parties in Munich's gay bars out of the newspapers. Nor could he be dissuaded from publicizing his behaviour, as when he insisted on pressing charges against a teenage rent boy who had robbed him although he had been warned that the case would attract adverse publicity. Homosexuality was nothing to be ashamed of as far as Röhm was concerned. He was proud of his sexual orientation, nurturing a homoerotic myth of splendid male physiques in battle and comparing his backstreet bruisers to the Spartan and Greek warriors of antiquity.

But his understanding or image of the proud homosexual

male was distorted by his own sadistic urges and addiction to violence. Röhm saw himself and his 'butch' cronies as the personification of hyper-masculinity and he disparaged effeminate men such as Hitler Youth leader Baldur von Schirach, whom he considered a 'hysteric'.

Fascism attracted men like Röhm because it extolled the myth of white male supremacy and the fallacy that 'real men' express their masculinity in exercising authority, domination and power over their supposed inferiors.

Whether Röhm had anything in that regard on Hitler, as other writers have suggested, is not known but Hitler evidently felt that he owed a great deal to his former army mentor, including his introduction to the party that he would ultimately take over, and for that reason Hitler was extremely reluctant to rid himself of the SA leadership until forced into doing so in July 1934.

Röhm's Role in Hitler's Rise

It was Captain Röhm who in September 1919 had ordered Hitler to attend a meeting of a new political party in Munich to assess its potential as a front for the army. Hitler duly reported back in his capacity as *Vertrauensmann* (the army's 'trusted representative'). He wrote in *Mein Kampf*:

> 'This was a time in which anyone who was not satisfied with developments . . . felt called upon to found a new party. Everywhere these organizations sprang out of the ground, only to vanish silently after a time. I judged the German Workers' Party no differently.'

The Deutsche Arbeiterpartei (DAP), or German Workers' Party, had been founded by railway engineer Anton Drexler and journalist Karl Harrer to campaign for workers rights, but neither had a talent for organization or oratory. They had attracted less than 60 members and were reduced to squabbling over the best way to spend the few marks that remained in the Party fund.

In *Mein Kampf* Hitler described the first meeting he attended in Munich's Sterneckerbrau beer keller.

> 'The minutes of the last meeting were read and the secretary gave a vote of confidence. Next came the treasury report – all in all the Party possessed seven marks and fifty pfennigs – for which the treasurer received a vote of confidence. This too was entered into the minutes . . . Terrible, terrible! This was club life of the worst sort. Was I to join such an organization?'

Hitler thought it was 'an absurd little organization', but his superiors saw the potential in the DAP for influencing the votes of former soldiers and workers and ordered him to join. The Party would be secretly funded by the army, which required influence over a political organization that could act as a front for it in its struggle against the communists, who were considered a threat to both the military and the state.

Röhm and his SA storm troopers became the Party's strong-arm security detail, ensuring that communists and other political opponents were prevented from disrupting meetings. And they made sure that Hitler had his way in dictating policy after he took over the leadership in July 1921.

Hitler therefore owed his political life to Röhm and for

that reason was forced to tolerate his openly homosexual activities until 1932, by which time the SA had grown into a significant military force of half a million men who posed a serious threat to the Reichswehr (the regular army). Röhm himself had become a liability and an obstacle to his protégé's political ambitions.

Ironically, had it not been for the political uncertainty that followed the Wall Street stock market crash of 1929, homosexual acts between consenting adult males would no longer have been a crime in Germany. Shortly before the financial crisis the Reichstag had voted to approve the Penal Reform Bill legalizing homosexual acts between consenting adults, but was prevented from approving it by the crash, which signalled the end of the Weimar Republic and democracy in Germany.

Hitler and Women

Whether Hitler had been an active member of the homosexual underground in Vienna, and later in Munich, during his youth as some writers have alleged, is impossible to verify. But it is undeniable that Hitler's intimate relationships with women were unusual and not a healthy experience for his partners, five of whom attempted suicide.

Eva Braun made at least two half-hearted suicide attempts in the early years of their relationship in order to secure his attention, British fascist 'groupie' Unity Mitford survived shooting herself in the head only to live the remainder of her life as an invalid and actress Renate Müller jumped to her death in 1937 before the SS could interrogate her about the accusations she had made concerning Hitler's 'unnatural demands'.

Initially Hitler would pursue women, but as soon as they showed any serious interest in a real relationship he would withdraw, becoming cold and indifferent. He clearly had a fear of intimacy which only surfaced when the object of his infatuation showed any interest in him. As a 17-year-old youth in 1906 he had fantasized about a young blonde, Stefanie Jansten, he had seen in the street in Linz, to whom he wrote poetry and a letter that he never sent. He didn't have the courage to speak to her, but imagined that they had an unspoken understanding, a condition known as erotomania.

Then in 1926, at the age of 37, he pursued 16-year-old Maria Reiter, who tried to hang herself when he turned his back on her after she responded favourably to his protestations of love. Evidently his volatile, prima donna personality was continually seeking turmoil and tragedy.

Geli Raubal

His second 'victim' was his young niece Geli Raubal (his half-sister's daughter), who shot herself in September 1931 because of what one of Hitler's early supporters, Ernst Hanfstaengl, called her uncle's 'twisted tenderness'.

Hanfstaengl observed a peculiar exchange between 'Uncle Adolf' and his teenage niece at the Schwarzwälder Café.

'. . . as they walked through the streets after the meal, Hitler emphasized some threat against his opponents by cracking the heavy dog whip he still affected. I happened to catch a glimpse of Geli's face as he did it, and there was on it such a look of fear and contempt that I almost caught my breath. Whips as well, I thought, and really felt sorry for the girl . . . I could not help feeling that her share in the relationship was under compulsion [. . .] She seemed to be rather cool towards him at times and manifested more fear towards him than fascination for him.'

According to one of Hitler's biographers, Konrad Heiden, Hitler had foolishly written a compromising letter to Geli in which he begged her to satisfy his masochistic cravings. When it came into the possession of an alleged blackmailer, Hitler asked a priest to retrieve it. The priest, Father Stempfle, was subsequently silenced on the Night of the Long Knives.

Nazi Party treasurer Franz Schwarz was said to have paid off several blackmailers who threatened to sell the secrets of Hitler's peculiar sex life to the press, including one who was in possession of pornographic sketches of Geli that Hitler was alleged to have drawn.

SA bodyguard Wilhelm Stocker later recalled:

'She admitted to me that at times Hitler made her do things in the privacy of her room that sickened her but when I asked her why she didn't refuse to do them she just shrugged and said that she didn't want to lose him to some woman that would do what he wanted.'

Disaffected former Nazi Otto Strasser suggested that there was 'something very unusual' about their relationship (apart from the fact that at 38 Hitler was twice Geli's age) and that Geli had spoken of being desperately unhappy because she could not do 'what he wants me to'. Strasser claimed that Geli confessed that:

'Hitler made her undress and that he would lie down on the floor. Then she would have to squat down over his face where he could examine her at close range and this would make him very excited [. . .] He demanded things from her that were simply disgusting. She had never dreamed that such things could happen. When I asked her to tell me, she described things I had previously encountered in my reading of Krafft-Ebing's *Psychopathia Sexualis* when I was a student.'

It has been suggested that her death may not have been suicide but murder and there appears to be some justification for those suspicions. The *Münchener Post* reported at the time that 'The dead woman's nose was broken, and there were other serious injuries on the body', which indicates a violent struggle.

> **WITH SOME JUSTIFICATION, IT HAS BEEN SUGGESTED THAT GELI RAUBAL'S DEATH MAY NOT HAVE BEEN SUICIDE BUT MURDER**

In addition, there is the curious fact of Geli's funeral. She was buried in a Catholic cemetery which the Church would not have allowed had she taken her own life. Even allowing for the possibility that the cause of death might have been withheld to avoid adverse publicity for the Party, it is revealing that the priest who presided over the funeral service, Father Johann Pant, fled to France. In 1939 a local newspaper published his allegations.

'They pretended that she committed suicide; I should never have allowed a suicide to be buried in consecrated ground. From the fact that I gave her Christian burial you can draw conclusions which I cannot communicate to you.'

Asexual or Impotent?

Once Hitler was in office, the threat of a visit from the Gestapo put paid to speculation regarding his sexuality in the German press, but the rumours persisted and when war came foreign correspondents would not risk having their press passes revoked merely to repeat scurrilous rumours and gossip. An exception was the Berlin columnist Bella Fromm, who wrote:

'I rather believe, and many people have felt the same way, that he is asexual, or perhaps impotent, finding a sexual sublimation through cruelty. They take private films of an especially gruesome nature in concentration camps. Films that only the Führer sees. These are rushed to him and shown, night after night.

'Occasionally Hitler's interest in a woman may be aroused; he may feel attracted by her charm, but that is all. His emotions culminate in a kind of jealousy caused by his sense of frustration, in the knowledge that he cannot respond normally.'

Hitler's Hair Shirt

'He is all genius and body,' was the Party line in 1930. 'And he mortifies that body in a way that would shock people like us! He doesn't drink, he practically only eats vegetables, and he doesn't touch women.'

Hitler's perceived virtues did not, however, arise from his devotion to duty or from self-discipline, but from his peculiar temperament. As an indolent youth he would frequently stay awake into the early morning haranguing his one and only friend, the forbearing August Kubizek, with his pipe dreams of future glory. He would become the architect of a new Vienna, designing imposing buildings to rival Rome, and he would live in a splendid apartment with a girl he had seen only fleetingly in the streets of Linz, and was infatuated with, but had never had the courage to approach.

He became a vegetarian only because he suffered from chronic digestive problems and had been advised to avoid eating fatty meat. He had also been persuaded to drink herbal tea instead of his customary flagon of strong Bavarian beer in order to quench his thirst and clear his head after an exhausting speech. As for the conspicuous absence of a female companion, there are numerous theories why Hitler avoided both marriage or a mistress, but conveniently for him and the Party propaganda machine the vacuous Eva Braun was willing to fill that function and not divulge the true nature of their relationship.

Whether Hitler's unusual routine of staying up until the small hours then sleeping in until noon was entirely due to his own peculiar habits is of little consequence, but the image he projected of tireless and selfless devotion to the Party and the nation was in stark contrast to the reality.

He abhorred real work of any kind because he knew he was incapable of seeing anything through. His indolent nature and lack of self-discipline had not hindered his ascent to power, but once in office it seriously impeded the day to day running of the administration. He shrugged off all responsibilities of the chancellorship by citing his belief that he was an artist and a genius and therefore excused from mundane matters, a fatal conviction shared by the sycophants in his inner circle. When pressed to attend to routine duties he would excuse himself by citing his favourite maxim: 'A single idea of genius is worth a lifetime of conscientious office work.'

But Hitler was no genius, despite what his acolytes might have told him and his assertion that the administration could function without him went unchallenged. The decisions he took were made on impulse as if divinely inspired, while other important decisions were delayed and trivial matters given undue significance and attention. Without direction from above, departmental reports were left unwritten, crucial meetings with the Gauleiters were not convened and the various ministries were left to muddle along as best they could while their Führer retreated to Munich or Berchtesgaden (a town in the Bavarian Alps above which Hitler built his mountain retreat, the Berghof), unwilling to enmesh himself in the routine of running a government. A disorganized, conflicted personality now reigned over an equally chaotic and competitive administration.

High Hitler

Later his erratic and unpredictable behaviour was exacerbated by his dependency on drugs. The official Party line was that drug addiction was a Jewish sickness and that drug addicts were 'criminally insane' and should therefore be imprisoned, or better still exterminated. It was an open secret among the press that Goering was a morphine addict, but foreign correspondents risked having their press passes rescinded if they alluded to it, while German journalists faced far worse.

Possession of non-prescription drugs was made illegal in Germany in 1933, despite the fact that the country was then a leading manufacturer and exporter of morphine and cocaine. Ironically, one of Berlin's most eminent chemists, Dr Fritz Hauschild, was then working on a formula for the mass production of a new drug that would re-energize tired *Hausfraus* and stimulate the work-shy into action. By 1937 he had succeeded in synthesizing a derivative of methyl-amphetamine-hydrochloride, which his employer, Temmler, patented under the name Pervitin.

The pharmaceutical company advertised it as a new wonder drug for restoring confidence and enhancing personal performance in everyone from secretaries to sportsmen and made it readily available without a prescription. It was supplied in tablet form and in glass ampoules for intravenous and intramuscular injection and it quickly became a huge seller. Women were by far the most eager consumers, particularly once word had spread about its dietary benefits. Amphetamine curbed the appetite and so led to fast and often drastic weight loss.

It soon became an essential supplement for soldiers, who found that it not only helped them stay awake and alert but also made them less susceptible to hunger, thirst, pain and the cold. Another side-effect was to increase the willingness to take risks, a benefit the military was eager to exploit.

In the summer of 1939 the Institute for General and Defence Physiology at the Academy for Military Medicine tested its effects on 90 university students and was satisfied it would make German soldiers more fearless. The director of the institute, Dr Otto Ranke, could personally vouch for its beneficial effects, having himself taken a sufficient quantity to stay awake for 50 hours at a stretch. Unfortunately for Dr Ranke, it also proved addictive, something which he presumably did not mention in his report. Ranke wasn't the only German doctor to succumb to the numbing effects of drugs during the war. By 1945 the cases of addiction among military physicians had quadrupled. In May 1940 Franz Wertheim, a German medical officer, admitted:

'To help pass the time, we doctors experimented on ourselves. We would begin the day by drinking a water glass of cognac and taking two injections of morphine. We found cocaine to be useful at midday, and in the evening, we would occasionally take Hyoskin. As a result, we were not always fully in command of our senses.'

Hitler's Drug-fuelled Army

After reading Ranke's report, the German High Command were cautiously optimistic, but insisted on a 'field trial' to evaluate the beneficial effects on soldiers under fire before they would approve its widespread use. The invasion of Poland in September 1939 provided the perfect opportunity. The first German soldiers to be given Pervitin were lorry drivers, whose unflagging energy and uncommon courage under fire demonstrated what could be achieved with a little chemical restorative.

In 1940, on the eve of the German blitzkrieg, the Wehrmacht and the Luftwaffe were supplied with 35 million tablets of Pervitin or its competitor Isophan and instructions that the stimulants be taken 'as needed to maintain sleeplessness'. In the event, between one and five tablets per day were taken by frontline troops and Stuka pilots and the surprise attack through the heavily forested Ardennes pressed ahead, rolling on remorselessly for three days and nights without the need for rest. Had it not been for the liberal use of the drug, the blitzkrieg of May 1940 might have ground to a halt.

However, it was only after prolonged use that the side-effects became known. Soldiers complained of suffering from circulatory ailments and profuse sweating. A few died from complications, but the benefits clearly outweighed the risks. Leonardo Conti, the Reich Minister of Health, attempted to have Pervitin's use restricted by the Wehrmacht but only succeeded in having it added to the list of restricted substances in July 1941 and a warning issued to the armed forces.

'Every medical officer must be aware that Pervitin is a highly differentiated and powerful stimulant, a tool that enables him, at any time, to actively and effectively help certain individuals within his range of influence achieve above-average performance.'

In January 1942, the remnants of a German battalion on the Eastern Front attempted to break through the Russians who had encircled them. The Germans were exhausted and suffering the effects of freezing temperatures. As they marched, the stragglers collapsed and were left behind to die. When darkness fell, the temperature plummeted and the officers decided that their only hope lay in giving the survivors Pervitin. The battalion doctor recorded that within 30 minutes 'the men began marching in orderly fashion again, their spirits improved, and they became more alert'.

But by 1944, Pervitin was not considered powerful enough to galvanize battle-weary and demoralized German troops into making that final supreme sacrifice for their Führer and Fatherland. A new 'super drug' was required.

The scientists who created it named it D-IX. Based on the Pervitin formula, it now included five milligrams of cocaine and five milligrams of the morphine derivative Eukodal (commonly used as a painkiller). It had been developed by the German navy who tested it on their midget submarine crews at Kiel.

These one-man U-boats were sufficiently small to avoid the anti-submarine nets that guarded the Allied ports, but they required the operator to stay awake for several days while they navigated through hostile waters. It was regarded as a last-ditch suicide mission with very little chance of the operator surviving, so the confidence-boosting properties of the drug were seen as being as crucial as its ability to keep the men awake.

Before they issued it to their crews the navy tested it on inmates at Sachsenhausen, where prisoners were forced to walk on a moving track until they collapsed from exhaustion. The moving walkway had been designed to test the durability of shoe soles. Having proven its effectiveness the new drug was then issued to the crews of the midget submarines, who were secured to their craft for 48 hours or more. Many suffered psychotic breakdowns during training and some of those who survived became disorientated before the mission could be completed.

Supplies Run Short

Towards the end of the war, after the factories producing Pervitin and Eukodal had been put out of action by Allied air raids, the drugs were in short supply and even Hitler appeared to be suffering from withdrawal symptoms. His hand shook, his once penetrating gaze had dulled and he shuffled round the bunker like an old man. An SS guard later said that he resembled a man of 70 and not someone of his real age of 56. His moods were also violently affected as he lurched from depression to rage from one minute to the next. It was thought that he might have been showing symptoms of Parkinson's disease, or the delayed effects of the neurological damage inflicted by the attempt on his life the previous July, but it looks more likely that the toxic cocktail of drugs was at least partly to blame. Chief among these was Eukodal (an opiate and forerunner of oxycodone) which produces a sense of euphoria. Hitler was having several injections of Eukodal a day, often combined with cocaine which had been prescribed for the pain in his ears following the failed assassination attempt at the Wolf's Lair.

The Dictator and the Doctor – Hitler and Dr Morell

Adolf Hitler was obsessed with his public image. A malignant narcissist, he dreaded what the crowds of adoring worshippers would think if they knew that their messianic leader was prey to chronic flatulence, which forced him to leave the room after every meal.

In 1931 Hitler changed his diet and became a strict vegetarian in an effort to find relief from crippling stomach cramps, but the pain persisted. By 1936 he was desperate to find a cure as the spasms were now accompanied by constipation, which he feared might be symptomatic of the onset of cancer, the affliction that had proved fatal to his mother.

Hitler's hypochondria originated in his childhood. His mother, Klara, had suffered several miscarriages and had lost three children in infancy. Consequently, she doted on her surviving son and his younger sister, Paula, fretting over Adolf whenever he became sick and instilling in him a pathological fear of germs and a morbid obsession with death.

The traumatic experience of watching his mother die while the family doctor looked on helplessly had led her son to put his faith in unconventional remedies and physicians.

By 1936 Hitler had acquired a number of personal physicians, but none had been able to identify the cause of his chronic digestive problems. None, that is, until he met Dr Theodor Morell. Morell had been recommended by Hitler's official photographer Heinrich Hoffmann, who was convinced that the physician had cured his gonorrhoea.

Morell had a reputation for treating sexually transmitted diseases using unspecified 'natural' remedies and also impotence using mild electric shocks. He had built a busy and profitable practice in a fashionable district of Berlin as a result. His clients included famous names from the theatre and cabaret as well as stars from the capital's UFA film studios – that is, if the framed autographed photos on his waiting room wall were genuine. It was hard to know what, if anything, was genuine regarding the mysterious Dr Morell.

He claimed to have graduated in Munich and to have served as a medical officer in the First World War, but he was wilfully vague when asked to name the ingredients in his 'vitamin compounds' and he frequently referred genuinely sick patients to other doctors, preferring to treat those with weight problems, 'social diseases' and impotence.

Hitler was not usually impressed by qualifications and was highly suspicious of orthodox science and learned academics. He preferred to rely on his intuition and instincts when judging people who might prove useful to him and when Hoffmann enthused about Dr Morell's unconventional cures, Hitler had a feeling that this was the physician he could entrust with his health.

As early as 1928, when he was 39 years old, Hitler had expressed the belief that he would die young and that he expected to live no longer than another 20 years. Less than 10 years later, he confided his fears to his architect and Armaments Minister Albert Speer.

'I shall not live much longer . . . for my health is growing worse all the time.'

This morbid obsession was not supported by a doctor's diagnosis for Hitler repeatedly refused a full medical examination, partly out of fear of having his own prognosis confirmed and partly out of concern for his image. It would not do for the 'Iron Man' of Germany to be seen to be prey to mortal weaknesses. To Hitler's relief, Dr Morell did not insist on a full medical examination (although Morell later claimed he had given Hitler a 'thorough' check-up).

Morell was more than pleased to go along with Hitler's wishes. An endorsement from the Führer guaranteed a steady stream of well-heeled clients to his consulting rooms. In fact, Hitler's refusal to submit to a full examination suited Morell just fine for he was convinced from their first meeting that there was nothing physically wrong with the Nazi leader. The episode of 'hysterical blindness' that Hitler claimed to have suffered as the result of a poison gas attack in 1918 only confirmed Morell's own diagnosis that Hitler was subject to psychosomatic disorders and that his chronic stomach cramps were another symptom of what Albert Speer described as Hitler's 'continuous inner turmoil'.

After a cursory examination, and on learning of Hitler's symptoms, Morell prescribed his natural 'cure-all', Mutaflor, which Hitler took on a daily basis for the next seven years. Mutaflor was a probiotic derived from the faeces of 'Bulgarian peasants', which would have been as beneficial as a placebo. Those patients suffering from psychosomatic ailments might find their symptoms relieved due to Morell's reassurance and their faith in his methods, while those afflicted with chronic symptoms but no serious underlying causes would have been no worse off. Morell simply couldn't lose. Unless of course he divulged the nature of his patients' ailments to anyone else.

Periodically the doctor would also subject Hitler to the spurious medieval practice of bleeding, using leeches to purge his patient of what he believed was his contaminated 'Jewish blood'. Since childhood Hitler is said to have been convinced that his paternal grandmother had been seduced by her Jewish employer.

> **PERIODICALLY THE DOCTOR WOULD SUBJECT HITLER TO THE PRACTICE OF BLEEDING, TO PURGE HIS PATIENT OF 'JEWISH BLOOD'**

(In 2010 one of Hitler's relatives, an Austrian cousin, gave samples for DNA testing which indicated that the dictator was not of pure Aryan blood and in all likelihood was distantly related to those races he despised.)

Hitler's Drug Dependence

By war's end Hitler was believed to have been taking more than 30 pills a day as well as injections including digestive remedies, tranquillizers, sedatives, amphetamines, cold preventatives, vitamins, anti-bacterial infection tablets, heart stimulants, bull semen extract for chronic fatigue and various forms of narcotic.

Concern for the Führer's health and his growing addiction to Morell's remedies were voiced by Hoffmann's former assistant Eva Braun, who became Hitler's mistress in 1932. She urged Hitler to bin everything he had been prescribed.

'He is poisoning you,' she told him.

Her pleas were ignored, for by now Hitler was an addict.

Braun had initially been in favour of Morell's 'natural' remedies, but she was soon repelled by his filthy personal habits, his dirty fingernails, his rancid halitosis and his evident neglect for his personal hygiene. She was not alone in describing his office as a pigsty and its morbidly obese occupant as a pig.

Dr Karl Brandt, Hitler's former personal physician, concurred with Braun, while Dr Koch, Albert Speer's physician, declared Morell 'incompetent' after having one of his gold foil wrapped compounds analysed. The laboratory reported back that the 'vitamin mixture' contained amphetamine.

Speer later wrote that Hitler's 'mistrust, hyperactivity, loquacity, agitation, loss of emotional control, capriciousness and irritability seem to have been the consequence of such treatment'. And that it was probable that Hitler had been taking 'these dangerous drugs' as early as 1936 and that by late 1942 it was a 'virtual certainty' that he was showing the symptoms of 'chronic amphetamine poisoning'.

In the original unpublished notes that Speer had prepared for his memoir *Inside The Third Reich* he noted the change in Hitler's behaviour from the summer of 1942 onwards, which he attributes to the diet of drugs. He remarks on Hitler's 'peculiar state of petrification and rigidity; apathetic uncertainty, agonized indecisiveness, an apparent inability to deal with all important problems and obstinacy when faced with them'.

The dictator became impulsive, irritable, prone to inner turmoil and subject to violent mood swings (from hypomanic to serious depression). Important decisions that were once made spontaneously were now delayed indefinitely to the frustration of those who waited to act on his orders. In private he would lapse into a state which 'often gave the impression of being mentally impaired' and 'frequently . . . confounding fantasy with reality'.

Speer recalled that Hitler would take 'countless Cola-Dalmann tablets' before giving a speech or taking an important conference. These tablets contained caffeine which compounds the effects of amphetamine. This would explain why Speer described the dictator as 'drunk' in the early hours of 1 January 1945 and in a state of 'permanent euphoria'.

Speer accused Morell of experimenting on Hitler while having no knowledge of what effect these drugs would have on his patient in the long term. This was a conclusion shared by Morell's bitter rival Dr Brandt as well as Brandt's colleagues Dr Hase and Dr Hasselbach, who were among the team of physicians who were at Hitler's beck and call. According to Speer, they considered Morell's methods 'unscientific' but they were never privy to precisely what he was prescribing. When questioned, Morell would offer a vague reply alluding to a 'special mixture' of vitamins and hormones.

Morell's reluctance to divulge the ingredients is understandable if inexcusable. These preparations were proving hugely profitable and enabled Morell to set up a manufacturing plant in Hamburg to provide Vitamultin, vitamin preparations and other dubious tonics as well as an anti-louse powder (Russlapuder) to the armed forces. As the money flowed in, Morell staved off paying punitive amounts of tax by investing the profits in the acquisition of more pharmaceutical factories that had been 'liberated' from their rightful owners in the German-occupied countries.

Brandt eventually took his concerns to Goering who initially showed little interest until Brandt read aloud from a medical textbook detailing the effects of strychnine poisoning. Goering agreed that the symptoms were alarmingly similar to the fatigue and mental rigidity he had witnessed in Hitler (as evidenced in his irrational 'no retreat' policy) and he confronted Hitler with Dr Brandt's accusation. Brandt was promptly sacked.

As for Morell, Hitler would hear nothing against his 'Dr Feel-Good' and was exhibiting the typical symptoms of an addict.

All the evidence points to the likelihood that Hitler was taking methamphetamine compounded in Vitamultin tablets and also as an ingredient of the daily Vitamultin injections, all of these prepared at Morell's pharmaceutical factory so as not to arouse the interest of the German drug control authorities.

Speer's View of Hitler's Dependence

Speer was adamant that whatever the nature of Hitler's chemical dependence, it cannot excuse him for his actions and for his 'monstrous, evil errors', specifically the persecution of the Jews, the establishment of concentration camps and the campaign against the Church, all of which had been set in motion long before he became addicted to Morell's mysterious 'remedies'. Nor can it account for his personality traits and characteristics, which were in evidence before the appearance of Morell and which were observed afterwards.

'Hitler was always inscrutable and insincere. He was always cruel, unjust, unapproachable, cold, intemperate, self-pitying; but at the same time he was the exact opposite of all that.'

Speer compared him to Robespierre, the reviled French

revolutionary leader who instigated 'The Terror' which saw thousands beheaded by Madame Guillotine. Like Robespierre, Hitler had a compulsion to deceive, according to Speer, a man who probably knew the German dictator better than anyone. He described Hitler as possessing a 'demonic' nature and as being a 'cold and unfeeling', ill-tempered man who avoided intimacy and probably loved only himself, but who could succumb to bouts of almost feminine sentimentality. In Speer's opinion, Hitler's fatal addiction was to power; Morell's cocktail of stimulants simply served as a substitute stimulant which in turn necessitated the tranquillizers to enable him to sleep.

Morell was among the last members of Hitler's coterie to leave the bunker. On 22 April he begged to be allowed to leave while there was still a chance to break through the encircling Russian lines and when permission was refused he fainted at Hitler's feet. Once in captivity, however, he claimed that he had been dismissed by Hitler for attending his brother's funeral without permission. Morell's brother was not a Party member.

Others describe being witness to Hitler accusing Morell of trying to drug him so that the Soviets could put him on trial.

'You think I am crazy,' Hitler is said to have ranted. 'You will try to give me morphine. Get out of here; you are sacked. Get that medical uniform off. Go home and act as if you had never had anything to do with me.'

Amphetamine Toxicity

All of the documented evidence together with the witness statements suggests that from 1942 Hitler exhibited the symptoms associated with neuropsychiatric illness, specifically rigid thinking, morbid anger, excessive attention to detail, the tendency to be easily distracted, pathological suspicion and elation. All of these afflicted him intermittently and impaired his judgement.

According to Leonard Heston, professor of psychiatry and co-author of *The Medical Casebook of Adolf Hitler*: 'The evidence is extremely strong in support of one basic cause for Hitler's psychiatric disability, amphetamine toxicity and no other diagnosis.'

Professor Heston analysed published descriptions of Hitler's erratic behaviour and archival records which listed several incidents of severe depression, as well as recorded episodes of hysterical blindness, chronic abdominal pains, headaches that went on for days, febrile illnesses, tremors, amphetamine toxicity, confused syntax and finally a stroke two months before his suicide. In addition, there was the discovery of Himmler's top secret report claiming that Hitler was suffering the tertiary effects of neurosyphilis.

Professor Heston and co-author Renate Heston, R.N., interviewed many of the people who had served under Hitler to gather first-hand testimony regarding his physical and emotional state as well as detailed descriptions of his behaviour and symptoms. These led the Hestons to conclude that: 'Hitler was intermittently incapacitated by organic brain disease with known signs, symptoms and predictable effects on behaviour.'

As for the theory that Hitler had exhibited the onset of Parkinson's disease in the latter months of his life, Heston argues: 'The chronic long-term administration [of amphetamine] perhaps combined with some physiologic eccentricity of Hitler's led to a total syndrome that had Parkinsonian elements.'

One curious discovery revealed by the surviving Morell

documents is that the doctor was prescribing uncommonly low doses of some drugs, so low in fact that they would have had no medical benefit. This suggests that he was doing so either to appease his patient or to be seen to treat him with something that he was not confident would have the desired effect. He was also injecting the dictator with glucose, which has no medical benefits but which would have been welcomed by Hitler if he believed it would combat fatigue. Secondly, Morell was at one time injecting Hitler with Strophanthin (digitalis) for a cardiovascular complaint that had not yet become so serious as to warrant it. In doing so, he was adding to the cocktail of chemicals in Hitler's brain and body merely in anticipation of a heart problem.

It is clear that Hitler was being injected up to five times a day with unproven and more than likely unnecessary medication as well as spurious vitamin concoctions. These injections saw an immediate and dramatic improvement in the patient, a recovery which was attested to by several witnesses and which, according to Professor Heston, could only have been attributable to amphetamine or cocaine.

Fortunately for history, we have a comparable incident involving Morell imposing the same treatment on a different subject. In March 1939 Emil Hácha, the president of Czechoslovakia, had been summoned to Berlin and presented with an ultimatum. Hitler demanded that Hácha capitulate or face invasion. Under extreme stress, Hácha collapsed and was given an injection by Morell. His recovery was immediate and he exhibited such nervous energy that Hitler later joked that he feared the ageing president might yet defy his threats and intimidation. It is revealing that Hácha asked Morell for a second injection later that day.

As Professor Heston notes, 'Amphetamine increases aggressiveness and risk-taking,' traits which characterized Hitler's behaviour from 1938 onwards.

The Hestons are not the only medical experts to speculate on the state of Hitler's health and the degree of his drug addiction. In 2010 historian Henrik Eberle and Professor Neumann of Berlin Hospital listed 82 different drugs known to have been taken by the Nazi leader in the 12 years he presided over the Third Reich, while also speculating that he may have had fillings formulated from gold torn from the mouths of concentration camp victims. Hitler would surely have objected to this on principle had he been made aware of it and yet his personal dentist possessed 50 kilos of gold taken from murdered Jews.

Mein Kampf – The Most Dangerous Book in the World

Adolf Hitler had the dubious distinction of having written one of the least-read, best-selling books of the 20th century, *Mein Kampf*. But it now appears that it may not have been the first book written by the great dictator.

Hitler dictated *Mein Kampf* ('My Struggle') to his devoted secretary Rudolf Hess while the pair languished in comparative luxury in Landsberg prison, west of Munich, following the failure of the Beer Hall Putsch of November 1923. The future Führer had been given a lenient five-year sentence by sympathetic judges, who had allowed him to use the court as a public platform to harangue the Bavarian administration he had attempted to overthrow.

In Landsberg, Hitler was allocated a spacious, well-furnished room with a view of the River Lech where he received a steady stream of visitors and well-wishers, who brought him flowers, chocolates and delicacies until his room resembled an opera diva's dressing room. With little to do but mark time until his release, he began to harangue Hess, his guards and anyone else who would listen with his angry and resentful rants against the 'November criminals' (the German republican politicians who had capitulated in November 1918) and those anonymous 'traitors' (a cabal of Jews, Marxists and 'cultural Bolsheviks') whom he imagined had 'stabbed Germany in the back' (using a phrase borrowed from General Ludendorff, joint leader of the German war effort in 1914–18).

Hess dutifully recorded these largely incoherent and rambling monologues until the Nazi Party's business manager Max Amann offered to publish them, provided Hitler agreed to rework his chaotic thoughts into a more comprehensible form. He would also have to consent to their publication under a more manageable title. The original 800-page manuscript laboured under the title, 'Four and a Half Years of Struggle Against Lies, Stupidity and Cowardice'. Amann abbreviated it to *Mein Kampf* and reduced the risk of losing his investment by dividing the book into two parts, each 400-page volume to be published a year apart, in 1925 and 1926 respectively.

Hitler was released on 20 December 1924 after serving just eight months of his five-year sentence and returned to find his party split by interfactional fighting. Amann had hoped that the Party's fortunes would pick up and with it sales of the book, but Hitler returned to find a demoralized party which had failed to exploit the nationwide publicity that his trial had generated. Consequently, sales of the first volume were disappointing.

A Collaborative Effort?

Despite Hess and Amann's best efforts to structure and shape Hitler's 'political philosophy', it still revealed the confused and often contradictory theories of a paranoid hysteric. Page after page was devoted to interminable, ill-informed tirades against a non-existent international Jewish conspiracy, punctuated with poorly argued justifications for an amoral doctrine of dog-eat-dog jungle law and interspersed with highly emotional denunciations of parliamentary democracy. Each part betrayed its author's morbid obsessions, with an entire chapter devoted to the subject of venereal disease and other sections given over to irrational and inflammatory arguments advocating the extermination of Jews as well as the 'humane' elimination of the 'weak' and the 'sick' in society.

As German historian Joachim Fest notes: 'With the anguished monotony of the insane, he returns again and again to these obscene fantasies . . . half concealed by that affectation of erudite moral philosophy in which pornographic works are accustomed to wrap themselves.'

A close analysis of the uneven tone and inconsistent reasoning suggests that the final version must have been a collaborative effort. It is believed that Hess had help from two rabidly anti-Semitic journalists, Father Bernhard Stempfle and Josef Czerny of the *Völkischer Beobachter*, as well as significant input from his former lecturer at Munich University, Professor Karl Haushofer, who had visited Hitler and Hess during their imprisonment.

The academic introduced Hitler to the theories of geopolitics and the concept of *Lebensraum* (living space), which were to be crucial in forming and rationalizing Nazi Germany's aggressive expansionist policies.

Equally significant was the advice the professor gave Hitler regarding his public image. Haushofer persuaded the Nazi leader to forsake his Bavarian lederhosen for a tailored suit or SA uniform and discard the riding crop which gave the impression that he was just another beer keller rabble-rouser. He also convinced Hitler to drink herbal tea instead of beer and coached him in the art of public speaking, which would enable him to project his voice and reinforce his arguments with appropriate gestures. Hitler would later have himself photographed in Hoffmann's studio striking these dramatic poses. The photographs would be sold as postcards to his Party acolytes and female admirers.

Meanwhile, sales of *Mein Kampf* rose and fell with the fluctuating fortunes of the Party, as they picked up votes whenever unemployment rose only to lose them again when the economy improved.

Required Reading

By the time Hitler succeeded to the chancellorship in January 1933 *Mein Kampf* was required reading for his legion of worshippers, though few could honestly say that they had actually read it in its entirety. Its poor grammar and turgid prose style led to it being commonly referred to as '*Sein Krampf*' ('His Cramp'). As Joachim Fest notes: 'Not one single sentence is free, relaxed and natural.'

It was pitted with grammatical errors and mixed metaphors ('the hard blow of Fate which opened my eye') as its author strained to substantiate his 'vulgarized Darwinian ideas' and make sense of the 'intellectual refuse' he had accumulated among the envious and embittered inhabitants of the Austrian dosshouses. Fest deduces that such mistakes reveal the 'fake scholar's ceaseless anxiety for applause' while the underlying tone of defensiveness betrays the fact that Hitler feared that his readers would not take his irrational and absurd theories seriously. Fest concludes that: 'The very fear of self-revelation is self-revealing.'

Hitler attempted to disown his work, disdaining it as 'fantasies between bars'. He told Hans Frank: 'If I had had any inkling in 1924 that I should become Reich Chancellor, I should never have written the book.'

Post-war surveys suggested that only a fifth of the population had struggled to read it from cover to cover and that many burned it after Hitler's death or used it for toilet paper during the privations of the immediate post-war period.

But every loyal Nazi was at pains to have it prominently on display in their home or risk being denounced by their neighbours. There was a gold-rimmed edition to be given to newlyweds (though few local authorities could afford to buy them), an edition printed on special thin paper for serving soldiers and even an edition in Braille for the visually impaired.

By the outbreak of the war *Mein Kampf* had been translated into 18 languages with total sales in excess of 12 million copies, making Hitler a rich man. He is thought to have accrued 12 million Reichsmarks in royalties. In 1934 he received a tax demand for 405,494.40 RM but he refused to pay, presumably on the grounds that he was chancellor and so would just have been paying himself.

Back on the Bookshelves

After the war the rights to *Mein Kampf* were assigned to the American occupying authorities, as Hitler had registered as a citizen of Munich which was then in the American sector. The Americans in turn transferred the copyright to the Bavarian government who prohibited publication for 70 years for fear that it might inspire a neo-Nazi movement.

Original copies were available in antique bookshops which required customers to provide their names and addresses and on loan under strict supervision from public libraries, which kept it in their so-called 'poison cabinet'.

It was finally published again in Germany in January 2016 in a heavily annotated 'scholarly' edition after its 70-year copyright had expired. The director of the Munich Institute for Contemporary History, which supervised the annotated edition, described it as 'a concoction of lies, half-truths and propaganda' while one of the team of historians said: 'It's a real feeling of triumph to be able to pick over this rubbish and then to debunk it bit by bit.'

While *Mein Kampf* was effectively banned in Germany, editions proliferated in other countries, from India (where it was used as a business instruction manual) to Japan, where a Manga version became a best-seller.

An early copy, autographed by its author, was auctioned for $64,850 in California in 2014.

Hitler's Autobiography?

Mein Kampf was part autobiography/part polemic, but it was not the first book to present its author as the messianic saviour of the German people. *Adolf Hitler: Sein Leben und seine Reden* ('His Life and his Speeches') appeared in 1923 and was credited to Victor von Koerber, but it now appears that its true author is likely to have been Hitler himself. Historian Thomas Weber, Professor of History and International Affairs at Aberdeen University, traced documents belonging to Koerber in a South African university archive which indicates the book was 'almost certainly' written by Hitler as a 'shameless but clever act of self-promotion'. Koerber had apparently been approached by the Nazis who sought permission to use his name and aristocratic background to lend the book credibility and to endorse its wild claims.

Its pseudo-religious tone asserted that Hitler was the messiah sent by Providence to save Germany and that the present work was the 'new Bible' of the neo-pagan religion he was to establish on Earth. Words such as 'holy' and 'deliverance' were peppered throughout, while Hitler's conversion to the cause of Aryan supremacy was compared to a spiritual revelation. Other passages are uncannily similar to several in *Mein Kampf*. Professor Weber found an affidavit signed by the publisher's wife stating that Koerber was not the true author and that Hitler had entrusted General Ludendorff to find a 'conservative' writer without a connection to the Nazi Party who would agree to lend his name to the book.

Other documents were unearthed during the search for the real author of the book, including a letter from Koerber in which he admitted to having given the Nazis permission to affix his name to a book he had not written. There was also a document dating from 1938 in which Koerber states that the book had been written 'with the active participation of Adolf Hitler'.

Double Speak and Double Standards

The Nazi leadership were masters of double speak and double standards. The regime advocated marriage and motherhood, but facilitated state-subsidized prostitution in the SS *Lebensborn* project, as well as in the concentration camps and – most notoriously – in the bugged Berlin brothel known as Salon Kitty which was frequented by Nazi diplomats, officers and officials. Many of Hitler's inner circle, most notably Goebbels, Himmler and Bormann, made no secret of keeping a mistress or two and, while Hitler himself was frequently seen in the company of the vacuous Eva Braun, it is likely that he encouraged the belief that she was his mistress merely to allay persistent rumours regarding his sexuality.

The duplicitous nature of the regime reflected the conflicted character of its leader.

Their opera-loving Führer and his Minister of Propaganda and Enlightenment, Goebbels, considered themselves cultured, but exulted in the public burning of books by some of Germany's most prominent intellectuals. At the same time Goering coveted stolen art and antiques primarily for their monetary value and the prestige that their possession brought him, while boasting that when he heard the word 'culture' he immediately reached for his revolver (a quote he had lifted from Hanns Johst's 1933 play, *Schlageter*).

In 1933 the regime outlawed homosexual acts between consenting adults and closed down gay clubs, citing Paragraph 175a of the Penal Code under which they persecuted, imprisoned and murdered thousands of homosexuals while harbouring numerous aggressively active homosexuals in their own ranks, particularly in the paramilitary SA and the Hitler Youth.

Paragraph 175a was also used to instigate false charges against members of the Catholic clergy when the administration sought to undermine the Church.

And in February 1933 they banned pornography, yet openly encouraged the odious Jew-baiter, sexual deviant and sadist Julius Streicher, who regularly published pornographic cartoons and articles in his racist rag *Der Stürmer* and who relished inflicting physical pain on his victims.

That year they also outlawed prostitution while soliciting prostitutes for both private parties and public events, such as the notorious 'Night of the Amazons' held at Schloss Nymphenburg and the infamous beer fests organized by Hitler's former bodyguard, Christian Weber.

In his memoirs of the period, *Munich Playground*, Ernst Pope recorded that the grotesquely corpulent Weber had been inspired to organize his nude carnival parades after visiting Paris and being impressed by the semi-clad women on display.

'Judging from what I saw in the French capital, our naked German girls are much better looking than the

French women. All we have to do is take the clothes off the girls right here at home, put them in the spotlight, and men with money to spend will forsake Paris for Munich.'

Pope also described the aftermath.

'Christian's carnival was a tremendous financial feather in his cap. I need hardly add that he also enjoyed the evening thoroughly. After the official part of the programme was over, I saw no more of the jovial sponsor. He disappeared behind the heavy red curtains of his private box, one of his self-selected chorus girls in each beefy paw. Christian has many children in Munich. If only he knew it.'

The regime which advocated 'traditional family values' had made a hero of a notorious procurer of prostitutes, Horst Wessel, celebrating his 'sacrifice' in the most memorable marching song of the period (for which Wessel's words were adapted to fit a popular folk song).

The 22-year-old Brownshirt leader had been murdered in January 1930 by a Communist Party activist, Albrecht Höhler, most likely in a disagreement concerning Erna Janicke, a prostitute that Wessel had procured for him, and was not a victim of a political assassination as the Party claimed.

Not surprisingly one of the most regressive, misogynistic regimes in European history condemned prostitution in public while its leaders indulged in extramarital affairs and paid for sexual services behind closed doors.

Treatment of Homosexuals

One irrational argument in favour of prostitution put forward by an anonymous Party official was that it discouraged homosexuality – the one 'vice', as they saw it, which the regime could not eradicate no matter how many individuals they sterilized or exterminated. Those who were subjected to sterilization were told they should consider themselves fortunate not to have been sent to a concentration camp where they would have suffered the prolonged agony of specious 'cures' at the hands of the camp doctors.

Classen von Neudegg, a survivor of Sachsenhausen, recalled that in the summer of 1944:

> 'Fear and uncertainty had arisen from rumours about new measures on the part of the SS hospital administration. At the administrator's order, the courier of the political division had requisitioned certain medical records, and now he arrived at the camp for delivery. Fever charts shot up; the sick were seized with a gnawing fear. After a few days, the awful mystery of the records was solved. Experiments had been ordered involving living subjects and phosphorus: methods of treating phosphorus burns were to be developed and tested. I must be silent about the effects of this series of experiments, which proceeded with unspeakable pain, fear, blood and tears: for it is impossible to put the misery into words.'

Despite the number of active homosexuals in the administration and the SS, the regime legalized the sterilization of homosexuals along with drug addicts, the mentally unstable, the physically disabled and the blind. Fifty-six thousand gay men were forcibly castrated within a year of the act being passed.

Himmler urged his officers to report any alleged offences of 'lewd and unnatural behaviour' or abuse within the ranks of the SS. By 1942 the dictatorship decreed that any male found guilty of a homosexual act would suffer the death penalty.

Lesbians were generally excluded from Party-sponsored persecution because it was hoped that they might still be persuaded into being inseminated by a virile Aryan and thereby contribute to the repopulation of the Reich. If they refused to volunteer for the SS *Lebensborn* stud farms, they would be forced to serve the regime in the state-supervised brothels.

Salon Kitty

As with any despotic regime, the members distrusted each other and would have turned on one another had they not been held in check by the man they both admired and feared, their Führer Adolf Hitler. In the spring of 1939, in the months leading up to the invasion of Poland, rumours were rife that there were members of the administration and the German armed forces that were willing to sell their secrets to their enemies.

It was primarily for this reason that Hitler sanctioned the establishment of the state-subsidized brothel Salon Kitty in Charlottenburg, a wealthy district of Berlin.

The apartments behind the elegant façade at 11 Giese-brechtstrasse had been refurbished at great expense, but Himmler, who had taken credit for the idea, hoped that the investment would be rewarded for he had ordered film cameras and bugging devices to be fitted in the walls to relay every sigh and unguarded confession to recording devices that had been installed in the basement.

Himmler entrusted the success of the operation to his deputy, SS Gruppenführer Heydrich, who took a personal interest in the project. Heydrich was head of the Reich Main Security Office (RSHA) which controlled the Gestapo, the SS Intelligence Service and the Criminal Police. Among the staff of the RSHA he was known as 'Himmler's Brain' due to his reputed intelligence, which by inference reflected poorly on his superior, but in the brothels and bars of Berlin he was known as the 'blond beast' for his reputed icy demeanour and his alleged predilection for violent sex, particularly when he was the worse for drink. He was also said to have kept a Jewish mistress, Josefa Huliciusova, a Czech whose existence was apparently known to his wife Lina. The Gruppenführer made frequent 'inspection tours' of Salon Kitty, which required him to sample the merchandise, but only after the hidden microphones had been switched off.

Madame Kitty's photo album listed the physical attributes and particular talents of her girls, who had been chosen to appeal to every taste. The majority were former prostitutes but among these were wealthy young women who had been persuaded that it was their duty to serve the Fatherland by encouraging their clients to talk candidly about their work, or to share gossip that might prove useful to the Gestapo.

Madame Kitty Schmidt (real name Katharina Zammit) had been 'persuaded' to co-operate after she had been caught trying to smuggle her illicit earnings out of the country. After being driven back to Gestapo headquarters in Berlin she had been interrogated by SS Obersturmführer Walter Schellenberg, chief of the SD, the Reich Intelligence Service, who suggested that she might prefer going back to her former profession rather than take early retirement in Ravensbrück.

Pillow Talk

Schellenberg did not approve of Frau Schmidt's way of earning a living, but it was his duty to loosen the tongues of military officers and Nazi officials whose loyalty was in doubt and he had come to the conclusion that there were more subtle and effective ways of achieving this. A man was more likely to let a secret slip to an attractive woman he was trying to impress, especially if he believed that it was safe to do so in the privacy of their bedroom.

> **MADAME KITTY'S PHOTO ALBUM LISTED THE PHYSICAL ATTRIBUTES OF HER GIRLS, WHO HAD BEEN CHOSEN TO APPEAL TO EVERY TASTE**

Schellenberg put his idea to Heydrich and he in turn took it to Himmler, who sanctioned the release of the necessary funds and gave his approval for the girls to be given appropriate training in basic espionage techniques.

Over the next few days hundreds of 'working girls' were rounded up by the Berlin police at the usual clubs, bars and brothels and brought in for assessment by a team of psychiatrists. Each girl was interviewed at length to determine their suitability and their 'emotional reliability'. Of these only 20 were selected for the training programme, which was held at an officer training school in Bavaria.

There they learned how to identify a client's military rank from his insignia as well as techniques for eliciting information without arousing suspicion. In addition they underwent an intensive course in several European languages.

When Salon Kitty reopened for business in March 1940 regular clients were provided with their usual partners, but if a gentleman used the prearranged code 'I come from Rothenburg' they would be asked to choose a girl from Madame Kitty's photo album. These men would be senior Nazi Party officials, high-ranking officers in the German armed forces and members of the diplomatic corps who had been told that the code would provide them with one of 20 girls reserved for special clients.

Among those invited to make their selection from the album was Count Galeazzo, Mussolini's son-in-law, who would divulge what he and the Italian dictator really thought of Hitler, whom Il Duce called 'that ridiculous little clown'. Such frivolous pillow talk made up the bulk of the 3,000 recordings transcribed for Himmler's eyes only, but occasionally their patience would be rewarded with information that was of military significance.

In the summer of 1940 Spanish Foreign Minister Don Ramón Serrano Suñer divulged the fact that his country intended to occupy Gibraltar, which would have threatened the German supply routes to Rommel's Afrika Korps. Consequently, the Germans drew up plans to seize the Rock without their allies' support, which if successful would have denied the British navy a shortcut through the Strait of Gibraltar, forcing them to take the long route around Africa. But a combination of factors prevented the plan from being implemented – among them the priority Hitler had given to the invasion of Russia and the lack of co-operation offered by General Franco.

The high-class brothel at Giesebrechtstrasse promised to provide the Nazis with more significant information, but it took a simple oversight to undermine the entire operation. British agents had had the building under surveillance from the outset.

In the winter of 1940 it had come to the attention of a British Intelligence officer, Roger Wilson, that many high-profile Nazis and familiar faces in the Party were frequenting this anonymous residential building that appeared to have no military or official function. Furthermore, workmen wearing brand new overalls were observed acting suspiciously while laying a thick multicore cable from SD headquarters in a neighbouring street to the brothel.

Wilson was then posing as a junior press secretary at the Romanian Embassy and was therefore able to use his cover to visit Salon Kitty to see for himself what was taking place and how the British might be able to bug the building themselves. Once he had confirmed his suspicions, it was a simple matter to tap into the wiring and listen in to everything picked up by the hidden microphones.

For three years the British overheard the intimate secrets of Nazi officials, including eavesdropping on Dr Goebbels' lesbian shows, but little of strategic importance is believed to have been gleaned before an Allied air raid in July 1942 put Salon Kitty out of business. When it finally reopened the SD saw no reason to return. Madame Kitty was allowed to move back in on the ground floor on the understanding that she kept silent about what had taken place at number 11 Giesebrechtstrasse. As for the 25,000 discs recorded in the basement, they are believed to be still under lock and key at the former headquarters of the East German security services.

Chapter Two

HITLER'S HENCHMEN

'Cryptic sciences, pseudosciences and frauds . . . The soil
was ready for the most absurd and lowest political mass
superstition. That was the faith in Adolf Hitler.'

Thomas Mann (novelist)

Like all criminal organizations, the Nazi leadership presented
a united front, bonded by a sworn loyalty to their leader
Adolf Hitler, but behind the scenes they detested each other.
Albert Speer compared the contest for Hitler's approval to
that of the Borgias.

'They were really very coarse individuals,' wrote Speer,
while singling out Goebbels and Goering as exceptions to the
rule. The latter pair of intriguers he considered 'very intelligent',
although Goering had been corrupted by his addiction to
morphine, while he judged Goebbels to be merely 'dangerous'.

Power Struggle

The bitter rivalry and infighting between the members of
the Nazi leadership was an open secret among foreign
journalists at the time. However, even they did not appreciate
how close the warring factions within Germany came to
deposing the dictator.

The Berlin correspondent of *The Spectator* reported on
23 February 1940 that within Germany there was 'growing

discontent and opposition' to Hitler among those who feared that the war might bring about 'a new and worse Versailles' should the Allies win. Such thinking would be silenced with the Fall of France, the occupation of the Low Countries and the routing of the British at Dunkirk that May, but in the months preceding the Nazi blitzkrieg there was significant opposition to Hitler's plans for conquest within the German armed forces. These various factions aligned themselves with leaders within the Nazi government who they believed could provide a 'more reasonable' face of the regime and who might come to 'an accommodation' with Britain to forestall a global conflict.

The German opposition was divided into two camps, the stronger one siding with Goering and the generals, and the other believing that the regime could only be toppled once the war was under way and Germany had awoken to the folly of following the dictator to inevitable defeat. In the view of the foreign correspondents, the latter group lacked a strong and decisive leader who could persuade the German people to support the removal of Hitler, while the former looked to Goering to take control once Hitler had been toppled and hoped that the Reichsmarschall could be persuaded to officiate over a 'more moderate' National Socialist administration.

The Spectator acknowledged that among the leaders of the Party a power struggle was taking place, whipped up by Goering and directed mainly against von Ribbentrop, Goebbels and Himmler. Goering was said to have the support of Deputy Führer Rudolf Hess, Reich Minister of the Interior Frick and others.

'The majority of the Generals, too, stand behind Goering, who has won over the leaders of industry and finance, and the intelligentsia. Since Goering is also the most popular Nazi leader among the masses, he is considered in all these circles as the man who alone can unite the German people. He also has sufficient force of character not to hesitate before any decision or responsibility, and can therefore see to it that internal reforms are brought about, and the abuses of the system removed.'

It was said that within the fevered atmosphere of Berlin ministries the main question was not what Hitler would do next, but what Goering might attempt, and whether he might succeed. For it was Goering who had been entrusted with implementing the Four Year Plan (to ensure Germany was economically self-sufficient) and by accepting the responsibility had become the de facto 'leader' of Germany.

The internal divisions were highlighted by the enmity between Goering and Nazi Foreign Minister von Ribbentrop, who had negotiated the non-aggression pact with Russia in August 1939 without Goering's knowledge and without consulting the military leadership. It was reported at the time that Goering let it be known that he would never forgive von Ribbentrop for this public slight and since then Goering had been 'working for Ribbentrop's fall from power'.

It was not only the thought of having been kept in the dark about this historic pact between Germany and the Soviet Union that rankled with the Reichsmarschall, but also the strategic blunder that von Ribbentrop had committed in giving Moscow both Norway and Finland in exchange for practically worthless guarantees of support against Britain and a free hand in southern Europe. Under the pact, Russia was able to establish a strategic base in the Atlantic on the Norwegian coast. In retaliation, Goering leaked the details of the deal before its official announcement to show von Ribbentrop in the worst possible light, for if the Russians had a naval base near the Finnish frontier and a presence on the Norwegian island of Spitsbergen it would pose a threat to the British navy and make any future peace overtures to Britain by Germany look like mere political posturing.

But while the enmity between Goering and the Nazi Foreign Minister was little more than a war of words, foreign journalists were filing stories that stated plainly that Goering 'wants to remove Goebbels, Himmler and Heydrich' from office. Goering and Goebbels were said to be 'old enemies', while the hostility between Goering and Himmler, and his deputy Reinhard Heydrich, stemmed from the fact that Goering felt that his authority and even his life were under threat because of the rapidly increasing power of Himmler and his secret police, the Gestapo.

It was reported in the foreign press that Goering was hatching plans to do away with Himmler and his deputy, just as he had removed Röhm in the Night of the Long Knives in June 1934. If Goering succeeded, it was thought that his popularity among the German people and his influence with the officer corps would benefit, for Himmler and the Gestapo were loathed and feared by both the masses and the German General Staff. The latter were known to have voiced their abhorrence at the atrocities carried out by the SS death squads in Poland the previous year and by the activities of the Gestapo within Germany itself. When Hitler took the salute of victorious soldiers in Warsaw on 5 October 1939 after the surrender of Poland, Wehrmacht officers physically distanced themselves from Himmler, who was left isolated and alone.

Joseph Goebbels (29 October 1897–1 May 1945)

'We shall go down in history as the greatest statesmen of all time, or as the greatest criminals.'

Joseph Goebbels

The Nazis originally presented themselves as a popular movement, a people's party promising 'work and bread' for the impoverished, but the socialist wing of the organization in northern Germany under Gregor Strasser was soon embroiled in a violent disagreement with the dominant group in the south led by Adolf Hitler.

The antagonism between the two elements came to a head in 1925 when all of the northern Party officials were summoned to a meeting. The northern Party officials accused the Munich contingent of corruption and pandering to the will of the industrialists who provided their funding.

Strasser demanded that the Party should stick to its socialist programme in order to attract workers away from the Communist Party and he also declared that the programme produced by the southern wing was confused and often contradictory. More significantly, Strasser's supporters objected to Hitler's imperious disregard for their opinion and his insistence that the Party should dismiss all notions of being a democratic organization and instead submit to the *Führerprinzip* (leader principle).

As the debate threatened to give way to violence, Strasser's secretary strode up to the stage and called for calm and then demanded the resignation of the 'upstart' Hitler.

'I propose that the insignificant bourgeois Adolf Hitler be thrown out of the Party!'

The speaker was Dr Joseph Goebbels, who would shortly

become Hitler's staunchest advocate. Twenty years later he would commit suicide with his wife after they had poisoned their children rather than live in a world without their Führer.

Goebbels considered himself to be a man of principles, but evidently those principles were for sale. By February 1926, Hitler could see that there was no avoiding a confrontation with Strasser and his supporters, and so he agreed to a meeting, but on his own terms. It would be held on a weekday when the majority of the members of the rival faction would have to be at work. Strasser, Goebbels and their supporters would then be in the minority and be intimidated by the presence of the wealthy industrialists.

At the end of that meeting Strasser and Goebbels had no choice but to withdraw their objections and pledge to back Hitler, who suspected that neither man would honour his promise once they had left Bavaria.

Strasser had been an early convert to the extreme nationalist cause, joining the NSDAP (National Socialist German Workers' Party) in 1920, a year after the party had been formed. He would prove to be a staunch and stubborn opponent until his murder during the Night of the Long Knives, which took place from 30 June to 2 July 1934. But Goebbels struck Hitler as someone who could be persuaded to abandon his principles for the right price.

Two months after the meeting in Bamberg, Hitler invited Goebbels to deliver a speech at the Bürgerbräu-keller, the symbolic seat of National Socialism where the Munich Putsch of November 1923 had been planned.

It was an invitation the conceited and unscrupulous former philosophy student could not refuse. Hitler shrewdly pandered to Goebbels' ego, receiving him like an honoured guest. After being driven through Munich in a limousine, Goebbels was booked into a suite at the best hotel. He was then feted by his Bavarian hosts and his concerns were listened to with practised politeness. By the time he returned to Elberfeld, Goebbels had 'seen the light', as he said in a fawning letter he later wrote to Hitler. He then publicly disowned Strasser in a malicious article published in the Nazi newspaper *Völkischer Beobachter*, an act of blatant political opportunism for which Hitler rewarded him with the position of Gauleiter (district leader) of Berlin.

> **GOEBBELS PRESENTED HITLER AS THE SAVIOUR OF GERMANY, HAVING HIS ENTRANCE ANNOUNCED WITH A FANFARE AND MARTIAL MUSIC**

The Orator

Goebbels proved his worth time and again during the subsequent campaigns. On one occasion, he circumvented the problem of having been denied a debate with an opponent, Chancellor Brüning, by playing a gramophone recording of a recent speech and interrupting it whenever he wished to make a point. It was a stunt that attracted columns of free publicity for the Party in all the major newspapers as well as making Brüning look foolish.

Once Goebbels had demonstrated his gift for staging such events, he was offered an active role in stage-managing Hitler's public appearances. It was Goebbels, more than any other personality in the Nazi leadership, who coined the familiar phrases associated with the Nazis and who created the image of the Führer that lingers to this day.

Goebbels presented Hitler as the saviour of Germany, having his entrance announced with a fanfare and martial music. The pomp and pageantry of ancient Rome that Goebbels had read about in his youth now became the setting for a comparable military empire, the Third Reich, which 'the little mouse general' proclaimed would last a thousand years.

Although in public Goebbels enthusiastically endorsed everything Hitler said, in private he declared that they were cut from a very different cloth.

Hitler believed everything he said, while Goebbels admitted that his own public declarations were made purely for effect. He had nothing but contempt for the masses and repeatedly said so.

As a young man he had been an avid reader and admirer of the Roman philosopher and political theorist Cicero, which had given his mother the idea that her son should enter the Church. But after Goebbels had enjoyed a heated discussion with the family priest it was decided that he was by inclination an atheist, and so was advised to choose another vocation. He would not find his God until he met Hitler.

Goebbels was devoted to Hitler but not the Party. The National Socialist credo of which Goebbels had once been a fervent advocate – which called for the nationalization of financial institutions, the abolition of interest rates and the redistribution of land to the poor – was cast aside as casually as he would discard his mistresses.

The Ram

Goebbels soon assumed the unlikely role of the regime's predatory seducer. Foreign correspondents remember that he fed them salacious details of his conquests in order to cultivate the image of an incorrigible ladykiller.

Even if he hadn't bedded all the women he claimed to have

seduced, he wanted to promote the possibility that he could do so in order to bolster his image and reputation.

Just as he had done in his youth, he used his intellect, superficial charm and caustic wit to impress a succession of women and to compensate for his physical deformity and evident inferiority complex. Himmler's loathing for Goebbels stemmed from the latter's pursuit of young film starlets and his shameless boasting of his conquests, which Himmler found to be morally reprehensible.

'Men of Dr Goebbels' type have always been alien to me,' the SS Reichsführer declared in 1939, 'though I have refrained from passing judgement. But today he is the most hated man in Germany. At one time we used to complain about Jewish managing directors sexually harassing their female employees. Now Dr Goebbels is doing it.'

Needless to say, if Goebbels didn't get his way he proved to be petty and spiteful. More than one actress found her career stalling after refusing his advances. He was a particularly vindictive man who once boasted: 'Hatred is my trade.' That hatred was rooted in rejection.

Like Hitler, Goebbels had been rebuffed in his youth after his plays had been rejected by theatre producers and directors and his attempts to find a job as a journalist had brought only rejection. And also like Hitler, he blamed others for his lack of success, projecting his deficiencies on to those he imagined had conspired to exclude him from his rightful and exalted place in the world. His malignant narcissistic personality simply could not accept his failings and he retreated into what is known in clinical psychopathology as 'the wounded self'. Only by striking back at those who had offended his inflated and fragile ego could he hope to cauterize that wound.

No slight would go unavenged; no questioning of his abilities would remain unchallenged. When rumours began to circulate that he was not of pure Aryan stock, Goebbels quashed them by having ethnology 'experts' devise a new category to explain his swarthy appearance. They classed him as a *'nachgedunkelter Schrumpfgermane'* (a dark dwarf-like German).

Luxury Lifestyle

Himmler made no secret of his deep disapproval of Goebbels' extravagant lifestyle and reckless expenditure, which included the acquisition of three substantial houses, a fleet of sports cars, a motor cruiser and a luxury yacht, all bought at the state's expense. The cost-conscious Reichsführer considered it to be a betrayal of National Socialist ideals. Nor was he fooled when Goebbels paid lip service to working class solidarity by insisting that his guests donate their ration coupons when they dined at his home.

Goebbels' primary residence, north of Berlin, comprised no fewer than five separate manor houses, the main house boasting 21 rooms, a private cinema, five bathrooms, electrically powered windows and an ultra-modern air-conditioning system. The total cost of construction was 2.26 million Reichsmarks, which in this instance was paid by UFA, the national film studio of which Goebbels had been made director. When the decoration and furnishings proved unsatisfactory, he simply drew the required amount from the budget allocated to other departments under his control.

To add insult to injury, 'the poison dwarf' flaunted his opulent lifestyle while professing to be hard done by. He told colleagues:

'If I were to spell out to you just how much I have to go without in my life because I am who I am, then I could prove to you that 80 per cent of the things other people can do, I myself am not free to enjoy . . . if I buy myself a new suit, I first have to check: Is this a Jewish firm?'

Less-publicized expenses included a regular manicure and lessons in social etiquette for this son of a factory clerk who had been embittered by a congenital deformity (the result of a failed operation on a deformed right foot) and his failure to fulfil his artistic ambitions.

In April 1936 Nazi Economics Minister Hjalmar Schacht attempted to curtail Goebbels' extravagance by recommending that Goering be appointed Commissioner for Raw Materials and Foreign Exchange. Schacht was sufficiently shrewd to realize that the only sure way to control Goebbels was to have him answer to his hated rival. Unfortunately, Goering was too indolent to keep an eye on Goebbels' spending and was unable to understand the most basic principles of economics, which made him the ideal candidate to manage the reckless Nazi economy.

By concealing his luxuries as legitimate expenses incurred during his official duties and having them paid for by the film industry, Goebbels was able to continue his profligate lifestyle free from Goering's interference.

Impossible to Characterize

But Goebbels' incessant boasting of his sexual conquests and his flagrant overspending and misuse of Party funds were not the only activities which invited criticism from his enemies within the Party. His rivals had long memories and had not forgiven him for the disastrous reception he had organized to celebrate the opening of the Olympic Games in Berlin in 1936. In a rare lapse of judgement, the Propaganda Minister had been persuaded to invite 'old comrades' from the early days of 'the struggle', SA thugs who soon got violently drunk to the horror of the assembled guests: the cream of Berlin society and numerous foreign dignitaries.

Himmler's assessment of Goebbels' profligacy and sexual exploits was shared by the general population, who were not taken in by the Propaganda Minister's feigned sincerity. When the live-in boyfriend of Czech actress Lida Baarova beat her Nazi lover senseless in the summer of 1937, the public revelled in the salacious details and thought it was nothing less than Goebbels deserved.

Those who suffered directly under Nazi laws were of course immune to his oily charm. The Jewish novelist Victor Klemperer had the measure of him when he wrote:

'He is the one educated man in the government, which is to say the quarter-educated man among illiterates . . . he is often called "the brains" of the government. If so, then the demands on him must be modest indeed.'

Goebbels was, however, a persuasive orator who was remarkably successful in persuading the masses that the introduction of anti-Semitic decrees and other measures to protect the state against 'the enemy within' were justifiable, but his anti-clerical campaign backfired and damaged his image in the eyes of the public. He had underestimated the depth of religious feeling among both the Catholic and Protestant communities, who reacted with revulsion when he attacked the Church with unfounded accusations of sexual impropriety and allegations of corruption.

Those who worked for Goebbels saw another side of him. Otto Jacobs, a stenographer in the Propaganda Ministry, described his boss as a man who 'never lost control' and was 'calculating' and 'ice-cold'. Others found him impossible to characterize. Dietrich Evers, a picture editor who worked on Wehrmacht propaganda, described him as always wearing the same poker-faced expression.

'It was impossible to see into Goebbels' heart . . . We just couldn't make him out.'

A Man of Few Friends

Goebbels was under no illusion regarding how his colleagues in the administration viewed him. He confided to his diary: 'I have few friends in the Party: Hitler is almost the only one. He agrees with me on everything. He will stand right behind me.'

This was far from a true picture of his relationship with Hitler. But then Goebbels wrote his voluminous diaries with a jaundiced eye on posterity, for he was secure in the knowledge that they would be published. He had been paid a 350,000 marks advance from publisher Max Amann, with which he purchased a country house outside Berlin. Even if he had not been assured of their publication, it is likely that he would have felt compelled to record his political and sexual conquests, if only to reassure himself that his distorted perception of reality was correct. He evidently believed in his own dogma that if a lie was repeated often enough it would eventually be accepted as a fact.

The Führer's secretary, Traudl Junge, was probably closer to the truth when she observed:

'Hitler admired Goebbels very much and rated his ability highly. But there was no note of friendship there. Hitler knew Goebbels' weakness: that he often exploited his position to get his hands on actresses. And that was utterly foreign to Hitler's nature.'

After Hitler had forbidden Goebbels to continue his affair with the Czech actress Lida Baarova the Minister of Propaganda found himself excluded from formal functions. If it had not been for the assassination of a junior Nazi diplomat in Paris on 9 November 1938 by a young Jew, Goebbels would not have had the opportunity to impress Hitler with a demonstration of his National Socialist zeal. In orchestrating the destruction of Jewish synagogues, businesses and private property on the Night of Broken Glass (*Kristallnacht*) Goebbels found himself readmitted to the Führer's inner circle, although it was an act which horrified other members of the Nazi leadership, who realized that they could no longer blame such 'spontaneous' outrages on hot-headed SA thugs.

Some of the Nazi leaders were enraged by the events of *Kristallnacht*. Himmler complained that his authority had been undermined by Goebbels' 'initiative', while Goering

GOEBBELS WAS A MAN 'WHO NEVER LOST CONTROL'... 'IT WAS IMPOSSIBLE TO SEE INTO HIS HEART... WE JUST COULDN'T MAKE HIM OUT'

was said to have thundered that his rival should have had the Jews murdered instead of destroying their property, as it could have been taken over by the government.

Hitler had no such qualms, but he was concerned that the regime's carefully cultivated image had been irreparably tainted in the eyes of its friends abroad. It would now be harder to claim that reports of Nazi persecution of German Jews in the foreign papers had been exaggerated by members of the 'Zionist' press.

Curiously, Goebbels had not expressed anti-Semitic sentiments until he met Hitler. As a young student at the University of Heidelberg he had been respectful of his Jewish professor Max Waldberg and had hoped to write his dissertation under the tutorship of the Jewish literary historian Friedrich Gundolf. He even had a five-year love affair, from 1922 to 1927, with a young school teacher, Else Janke, who was half-Jewish and though he may have suspected that the theatre directors and producers who had rejected his plays were Jewish, he did not refer to their religion when he spoke bitterly of those times.

It is significant that he only inserted anti-Semitic material into his unpublished semi-autobiographical novel *Michael* when the official Nazi publishing house offered to print it. He appears to have adopted a violent anti-Semitic attitude in the late 1920s only to comply with Hitler's wishes and to rant in unison with his idol.

Such feigned devotion did not impress the other members of the Nazi hierarchy, who sniggered when they heard that Goebbels planned to name his children in honour of 'Onkel Adolf' (Helge, Hilde, Helmut, Holde, Hedda and Heide). In their eyes such blatant toadying was beneath contempt.

Master of Manipulation

Goebbels was a firm believer in the maxim that 'any publicity is good publicity'. While some in the Party voiced concern regarding the violence that broke out at meetings between the SA and communist agitators, Goebbels persuaded Hitler to let the SA thugs break a few heads if they wished, as he knew the publicity would attract the sort of new members who were keen to see some action.

When the violence attracted the attention of the Berlin authorities, the Nazis were banned from holding public meetings in the capital for two years. Goebbels, however, would not be silenced. He announced the publication of a weekly Party newspaper, *Der Angriff* ('The Attack'), with a teaser poster campaign that bore only the title and a question mark to ensure it swiftly became a topic of conversation.

The fiercely anti-Semitic articles and crude political cartoons were deliberately provocative, denigrating the Berlin police, vilifying the communists and ridiculing the Weimar government, which the Nazis accused of being ineffective and impotent.

Beginning as a weekly in 1927, with an initial print run of 2,000 copies, by the winter of 1930 the paper had become a daily with a circulation in excess of 100,000. Three years later, after the Nazis had seized power, they owned two-thirds of all periodicals published in Germany and dictated the editorial policy of the three leading newspapers, which they allowed to remain independent to give the impression that they were impartial.

As Minister of Propaganda and Enlightenment, Goebbels was able to feed the press with stories the regime wanted publicized in the manner in which they wanted to present them. Nothing was printed without his approval. His memo to editors on 22 October 1936 was a thinly veiled threat to those journalists who still imagined they could write what they wanted:

> 'It turns out time and again that news and background stories still appear in the German press which drip with an almost suicidal objectivity and which are simply irresponsible. What is not desired is newspapers edited in the old Liberalistic spirit. What is desired is that newspapers be brought in line with the basic tenets of building the National Socialist state.
>
> 'What is necessary is that the press blindly follow the basic principle: The leadership is always right!'

All media employees were vetted and those known to have socialist sympathies were dismissed. The remainder were required to submit their reports and articles to the state-controlled press agency, the DNB, for approval. Criticism of the regime was strictly forbidden.

CENSORSHIP SMOTHERED FREE SPEECH IN EVERY FORM. EVEN POPULAR ENTERTAINMENT WAS BLIGHTED WITH NAZI PROPAGANDA

Censorship smothered free speech in every form. Even popular entertainment was blighted with Nazi propaganda. The national film company, UFA, was informed that it would have to comply, or be closed down. Under Goebbels the film company produced a number of virulent anti-Semitic films, of which *Jud Süss* ('Süss the Jew') (1940) was by far the most notorious. But Goebbels knew that an unremitting diet of propaganda was likely to instil resistance in a population that needed to escape from reality – from

The Hitler Youth organization was conceived as a way of indoctrinating boys and young men (from 10 to 18 years old) to the cause of the Third Reich. By 1936, there were around 4 million members. Hitler said: 'A young German must be as swift as a greyhound, as tough as leather and as hard as Krupp steel.'

Magda and Joseph Goebbels were married in 1931 in Mecklenburg, northern Germany. The marriage had Hitler's blessing – he was best man – and Harald Quandt, Magda's son from her first marriage, can be seen in the uniform of the *Deutsches Jungvolk*, or junior Hitler Youth. Magda and Joseph had six children, five girls and a boy, but Harald outlived them all. Magda and Joseph ordered his six half-siblings to be murdered in Hitler's bunker just before Berlin fell.

Adolf Hitler in a rare unguarded moment in the company of his niece Geli Raubal. He clearly felt relaxed with her, but did they have a perverse sexual relationship, and was he responsible for her death and a subsequent cover-up?

Bundesarchiv

Ernst Röhm (facing camera) was a co-founder of the
Sturmabteilung (SA), the thuggish, street-fighting arm of
the Nazi Party. He became their chief of staff in 1931.
That same year, the *Münchener Post*, a Social
Democratic newspaper, published personal
correspondence from Röhm that showed him to be
homosexual. His close friendship with Hitler – they called
each other *du* – led to rumours that Hitler was gay.

A harshly lit portrait of Hermann Goering from August 1932 to celebrate his appointment as President of the Reichstag. The medal he wears is the 'Blue Max', or 'Pour le Mérite', awarded for his exploits as a fighter pilot in the First World War. As a top government official, Goering was now in a position to indulge his taste for luxury, inflating his income through bribery, corruption and the confiscation of Jewish property.

In January 1933, Hitler became Chancellor; in April, the Gestapo was established. In this way, the Nazis began to ratchet up their domestic reign of terror. Here, sadistic members of the Navy SA pose with their victims as they denounce a woman and her Jewish boyfriend in front of the local Nazi HQ, Cuxhaven, north Germany.

A Jewish boy is made to cut his father's beard at the instigation of jeering German troops, 1933.

Nazi women pass by in formation at the opening of the Adolf Hitler Sports Stadium, Stuttgart, 1933. Nazi puppet-masters loved to choreograph the German people into moving patterns which suggested order and control, and with costumes that linked them to a glorious mythical past. The idea was to show participants dancing to the Führer's tune – obedience training that could be broadcast around the world.

The figure of Hitler spotlit in a window of the Chancellery in Wilhelmstraße, Berlin, after winning the election of 1933. He saw himself as a man whose time had come.

Clutching the *Blutfahne* (bloodflag), the notorious Julius Streicher leads 'old comrades' in commemorating the Munich Putsch. The failed Putsch of 1923 had been little more than a pointless scuffle with Bavarian police during which 16 Nazis were killed, but Hitler kept mining it for political capital. After all, the trial which had followed it had put him centre-stage in German politics.

Drunk on power, Hitler exhorts members of the
Hitler Youth at Nuremberg in 1934. Rudolph Hess
can be seen just behind him in the background.
Hess was Hitler's warm-up man, leading the
audience in reciting the official oath of allegiance
to the Führer – it's rumoured that Hitler drafted
the words himself. Millions of soldiers and civil
servants bleated them back between 1934 and
1945, and thereby allied themselves to their
Führer and to his fate!

increasing restrictions, rationing and the relentless Allied air raids – and so he commissioned a stream of sentimental melodramas and romantic musicals extolling Aryan values and the virtue of self-sacrifice for family and the Fatherland.

Intellectual Warfare

Radio, too, was exploited to spread the message to the masses. Thousands of cheap wireless sets officially called the *Volksempfänger* ('people's receiver'), but more commonly known as 'Goebbels' snout', were manufactured under a state subsidy so they could be sold for as little as 35 marks, ensuring that almost every home could afford one. Albert Speer estimated that by 1939 70 per cent of the population tuned in to hear their Master's Voice: the voice of the Führer or that of his mouthpiece, Dr Goebbels.

Every official announcement was carefully orchestrated and planned to ensure that as many as 80 million listeners would be tuned in when the news was broadcast. Housewives and the elderly were seen as a captive audience in their homes, while workers were subjected to piped music interspersed with propaganda in department stores, offices and factories.

After work and at weekends the incessant indoctrination process continued from wireless sets installed in bars, cafes and other public meeting places. Announcements were timed to allow housewives to interrupt their chores and mothers to quieten their children. It was all part of a campaign Goebbels called 'intellectual warfare'.

Of course there were clear restrictions to what the listener could listen to.

The two-band sets could only receive signals from local

and regional stations or the state mouthpiece, RBC. Reception was too weak to pick up overseas broadcasts.

But although Goebbels embodied the official voice of the regime, privately he expressed serious concerns regarding Hitler's war aims. He did not share his Führer's belief that they would see a swift and decisive victory for Germany and he became even more pessimistic when the Russian campaign turned against Germany in the summer of 1943.

It was then that he urged Hitler to come to terms with Stalin, even though it would mean withdrawing from the occupied territories in the East. Hitler refused to do a deal with 'the Bolsheviks' and Goebbels was forced to face the stark possibility that the best he could do was delay the inevitable. In a newspaper article 'The Year 2000', he predicted that, if Germany was defeated, the Allies would divide Europe between them and that an 'iron curtain' would separate the former Allies.

When the Allied air raids began Goebbels attempted to stiffen the population's resolve by denouncing them as 'terror attacks' and when Hitler and the other Nazi leaders refused to be seen in the rubble-strewn streets Goebbels made publicized appearances among the ruins. He believed that by doing so he strengthened Germany's determination to fight to the bitter end.

Spin Doctor

Though Goebbels never gave Hitler reason to doubt his loyalty, he was rarely taken into the Führer's confidence regarding his plans for conquest. In the months preceding Operation Barbarossa, the invasion of the Soviet Union on 22 June 1941, Goebbels was kept in the dark. In the winter of 1940 he vented his frustration in his diary.

'Sooner or later we must settle matters with Russia. When I don't know, but I do know it will happen.'

Hitler only informed his Propaganda Minister when he needed Goebbels to disseminate false rumours of a diversionary attack in the west against Britain.

Hitler turned to Goebbels again when the German advance ground to a halt barely four weeks after the invasion. He looked to 'the brains' of the Third Reich to explain how the infallible conqueror and self-styled military genius had been misled as to the strength of the Soviet forces and their weaponry. Goebbels then demonstrated his talent in times of adversity – he lied with complete conviction. Using the newspapers, radio broadcasts and cinema newsreels, Goebbels predicted imminent victory over the 'subhuman Bolshevists'.

His masterful handling of the humiliating defeat of the German army at Stalingrad in February 1943 staved off an attempt by Himmler to take over the Propaganda Ministry and earned him the grudging respect of a besieged and increasingly disillusioned citizenry. Goebbels, they said, had told them the unvarnished truth; that even the once invincible German army could not always be victorious and that sacrifice in time of war was inevitable, even necessary.

But even when faced with the crushing defeat in the East, the arch Nazi spin doctor shamelessly drew on the *schmaltzig* myth of heroic sacrifice.

'The army of the dead has not surrendered its weapons,' he told them in a *Sondermeldung* ('special announcement'), broadcast after playing a recording of the sentimental song 'I Had Some Comrades'. 'It marches along with the ranks of the German soldiers.'

Goebbels urged Hitler to make a similar speech to rally

the people after the shock defeat, but Hitler refused to appear in public and admit what he could not bring himself to accept. So Goebbels was left to make the speech of his life on 18 February 1943 at the vast Berlin Sportpalast, one in which he called for 'Total War' to stem the tide of Bolshevism. Needless to say, the crowd roared their assent, leaving Goebbels to joke: 'If I had ordered them to jump out of the window they would have done so!'

Unknown to the audiences who viewed the newsreel in the cinemas later that week, the crowd at the stadium comprised hundreds of loyal Party members drafted in to cheer the speech.

Hermann Goering (12 January 1893–15 October 1946)

Goering's rivals within the regime were brutal in their assessment of the Reichsmarschall, with Goebbels referring to him as 'a fat slob' and a 'repulsive old roué', in reference to his habit of wearing make-up and lounging around in silk dressing gowns in a poor imitation of composer Richard Wagner.

'He is a liability to the Party,' he went on. 'Added to which he is as thick as two planks and bone idle.'

Goering, in turn, considered his acid-tongued adversary to have no genuine opinions or beliefs that he could profit by. Goebbels, he said, was 'too much of a thief and a dishonest opportunist to have any deep-seated feelings for or against anything . . . he was so dishonest that it didn't pay to discuss anything with him'.

Goering may have cultivated the image of a jovial, Falstaffian figure, but he was not a man one could afford to cross. Even after Hitler had transferred responsibility for the running of the concentration camps and the Gestapo to Himmler in 1934, Goering continued to spy on his rivals. As head of the Research Office of the Air Ministry, he authorized the bugging of telephones in Party offices, ministries, embassies and even the Reich Chancellery. The information he collected in this way proved crucial in the weeks leading up to the Röhm purge, but Goering soon tired of political infighting once his prestige was on the wane and he retreated to his palatial country estate outside Berlin.

Reichsmarschall Hermann Goering wallowed in a ludicrously idealized image of himself as 'the last Renaissance man'. The portly former head of the Gestapo and commander-in-chief of the Luftwaffe saw himself as a jolly avuncular figure and a man of the people. His rivals in the regime, however, viewed him in an entirely different and unflattering light.

Foreign diplomats who had had the misfortune to lock horns with 'the Fat Man' in the pre-war years were equally disparaging. The French Ambassador to Germany, André François-Poncet, accused Goering of being 'cunning', 'cold-blooded' and 'cruel', while his successor Robert Coulondre observed: 'Goering is as ridiculous as he is dangerous.'

Coulondre was alluding to Goering's ambitions to build a formidable air force in defiance of the Versailles Treaty and in flagrant disregard of the ruinous effect it would have on the German economy. But Coulondre was also aware of Goering's role in the resignation of Hjalmar Schacht, the Reich Minister of Economics and President of the Reichsbank, in December 1937 as well as the part he had played barely a month later in plotting the downfall of the Minister of War, Werner von Blomberg, whose post he had coveted.

It would have been a simple matter for Goering to have forced the resignation of Blomberg, who had scandalized polite society by marrying a former prostitute, but that would not have guaranteed him the position. He would first have to sideline his likely replacement, Baron von Fritsch, commander-in-chief of the army. By simply accusing Fritsch of conduct unbecoming an officer (on a trumped-up charge involving a homosexual prostitute) he compelled him to resign. However, Goering had not foreseen that Hitler would then assume the role himself and palm him off with another vacuous title, that of Feldmarschall, an honorary rank with little authority over the German General Staff.

Nevertheless, Hitler could not afford to alienate the one man in his administration capable of command. On the day Germany invaded Poland, Hitler named Goering as his successor and six months later, following the defeat of France and the Low Countries in May 1940, he appointed Goering Reichsmarschall, with seniority over all officers in the German armed forces.

Morphine Addict

However, Goering's notorious brusqueness and his habit of bullying both his pilots and his ministerial staff did not endear him to his subordinates. General of the Luftwaffe Helmuth Förster held his superior in little regard, accusing him of being a 'pathetic morphine addict' who would fall asleep in a meeting after the effects of the drug had worn off.

Goering's addiction originated in 1923 after he had sustained a bullet wound to the groin during the failed Munich Putsch, when Hitler and his SA thugs had attempted to overthrow the

Bavarian government. The injured Goering had escaped imprisonment by fleeing first to Austria and then to Sweden with his first wife, Carin von Kantzow, the daughter of a Swedish baron. There he was diagnosed with a severe nervous disorder and admitted to Långbro mental nursing home, where he spent five weeks from 2 September to 7 October 1925 under observation.

His medical report described him as a highly emotional and 'disruptive' patient; a self-centred hysteric suffering from a persecution complex who was plagued with visions and voices. He attacked staff and attempted suicide on several occasions. He was also said to possess an 'exaggerated self-confidence' when not berating himself over his failures.

By that time he was injecting himself on an almost daily basis with a morphine derivative and was soon a bloated caricature of his former self. But he was either unwilling or unable to wean himself off the drug and was continually castigated by his wife for his habit and lack of willpower. It was an assessment supported by one of the doctors, who accused the recalcitrant patient of lacking 'fundamental moral courage'.

Early Days

On his release, Goering attempted to get back on the straight and narrow with a job selling aircraft engines, but was readmitted to the clinic on 22 May 1926 for a further month, after which he declared himself cured. He then returned to Germany under an amnesty for those accused of political offences and took up with Hitler once again.

Goering was then suffering from chronic insomnia and was piling on the weight despite an addiction to slimming pills. Hitler, however, considered his aristocratic background and polished social skills to be an asset to the Party, not to mention his enviable military record with Baron von Richthofen's squadron, during which he had been awarded a Blue Max (*Pour le Mérite*) for downing more than 20 British planes. But the official record may not have reflected the facts. It was alleged that Goering had only shot down 15 enemy fighters. Nor did his file mention the time he had forged papers authorizing his transfer from his infantry regiment to a flying school, nor the fact that he had narrowly escaped a court martial for doing so owing to the intervention of his Jewish godfather, Dr Hermann von Epenstein.

Goering's mother had been Epenstein's mistress for 15 years and during that time her brood had enjoyed a life of luxury in her lover's castle at Mauterndorf. There they had been waited on by a small army of servants and serenaded by minstrels. Later they would live in Veldenstein castle near Nuremberg, again as guests of Epenstein until he discarded Frau Goering for a younger woman. But it had been an idyllic time and one to which the adult Goering yearned to return.

Thereafter Goering felt entitled to live the life of an aristocrat, even though he had been born without a title and had not earned one.

Carinhall

By the time the Nazis stormed to power in 1933 Goering had the means to purchase Carinhall, a 100,000-acre country retreat at Schorfheide, north of Berlin, where he could play the Lord of the Manor, strutting through the grounds dressed in a leather hunting outfit and carrying a bow and arrow. He considered himself a courageous big game hunter, but his guests recall that he would sit in a hide for hours waiting for his prey to come within range of his gun or bow.

Although he enjoyed stalking and killing defenceless animals, he apparently took his responsibilities as *Reichsjägermeister* and *Reichsforstmeister* seriously, replenishing the surrounding forests with moose imported from Sweden and bison from North America. He also instigated a programme for the renewal of deforested regions and tightened the hunting laws to ensure that there were sufficient numbers of birds and wild animals for his fellow hunters to slaughter.

Carinhall had been named in memory of Goering's first wife, whose body he had ordered to be exhumed and reburied in the grounds so that he could continue to worship her, to the consternation of his second wife, German actress Emma Sonnemann, or 'Emmy' as she was known.

Emmy was married when they met and mother to a nine-year-old son. Their church wedding in Berlin on 10 April 1935 was stage-managed to demonstrate the might of Goering's Luftwaffe, which flew overhead in close formation while thousands of troops marched past to take the salute. Hitler agreed to be best man in a ceremony which lasted barely ten minutes, but he was known to loathe Emmy, whom he described as 'the cancer within Goering'. Hitler blamed her for 'softening' his once pitiless and cold-blooded comrade and thereafter referred to his former right-hand man as 'an old woman'.

The manor house at Carinhall had been designed by architect Werner March, who had planned the Berlin Olympic stadium. But it was never large enough to satisfy its owner or his enormous ego.

A study was constructed with a domed ceiling modelled on the Vatican Library and this was furnished with an imposing 25-foot-long desk, studded with precious gems and inlaid with bejewelled swastikas. Further enlargements were made to the main house and new facilities were added, including a tennis court and an indoor swimming pool.

The manor house was also host to a priceless art collection to rival that of the great museums and galleries of Europe, which was not surprising as Goering had acquired the choicest pieces in his collection from those same galleries as well as from some of the finest private collections in Germany, Holland and France, having made the owners an offer they couldn't refuse.

Five priceless portraits by Rembrandt hung on the walls, alongside masterpieces by Goya, Rubens, van Dyck and Velázquez. Classical Graeco-Roman statues stood in the grounds that would not have been out of place at the Palace of Versailles and valuable Gobelin tapestries lined the walls, with hunting trophies, armour, medieval weapons and antiques completing the scene of baronial grandeur. It was a magnificent setting in which to host Goering's celebrated lavish parties, with food fit for a king served on gold-rimmed plates and eaten using solid silver cutlery engraved with Goering's fictitious coat of arms.

A 'Perfumed Nero'

Until the very end his envoys were returning from the occupied territories with plunder, antiques and art, until even the vast rooms of Carinhall and his other country estates were teeming with treasure. When he finally gave the order to evacuate Carinhall prior to its demolition on 28 April 1945, the entire collection was hastily packed into a convoy of trucks and taken to the railway sidings. It was then loaded on to a train bound for Berchtesgaden, where Goering hoped he and his precious possessions would avoid falling into the hands of the advancing Russians. There it was carefully unloaded and stored in a Luftwaffe facility. The paintings alone occupied 14 rooms, the statues

GOERING'S PAINTINGS ALONE OCCUPIED 14 ROOMS, THE STATUES ANOTHER FOUR, AND OTHERS WERE PACKED WITH CRATES OF VALUABLE CHINA

another four, and others were packed from floor to ceiling with crates of valuable china. Even the chapel had to be cleared of pews to accommodate his hoard of Renaissance furniture.

The German public had little idea of the luxurious lifestyle their leaders were indulging in, although they were aware that each member of Hitler's inner circle owned a magnificent private villa in Berlin and another equally opulent summer residence on the Obersalzberg. (This beautiful mountain retreat, where Hitler also lived, was situated above the town of Berchtesgaden.) Also, many had seen Goebbels attending film premieres with gorgeous young starlets on his arm and Goering posing for pictures in the grounds of his estate for the newsreels and magazines, like some Hollywood film star. However, the public perception, at least in Germany, was that Goering was no more corrupt than any other politician and that he evidently enjoyed his beer and food as much as the average Bavarian male. He was not perceived as a threat, unlike Goebbels, who was generally regarded with suspicion. But those who caught the Reichsmarschall behind closed doors saw a conceited, shamelessly self-indulgent and debauched figure, a 'perfumed Nero' as one witness saw fit to describe him.

Swiss diplomat Carl Burckhardt witnessed Goering reclining

on an ottoman with his trouser leg rolled up to the knee, exposing red silk stockings 'like a Cardinal', with a petulant look on his bloated face, his mouth 'sunken and puckered like an old woman's'. Another guest, German diplomat Ulrich von Hassell, noted that Goering would change his outfit several times a day, often appearing in a kimono or a Roman-style toga fastened with a gold clasp and fur-lined bedroom slippers at dinner, his sausage-like fingers encrusted with ostentatious rings. Others recalled seeing him attired in a velvet jacket, ruffled shirt and knickerbockers with gold buckled shoes, the image of a bloated little aristocrat.

Self-pity

The opulent lifestyle he enjoyed at Carinhall is well documented, but Goering acquired other palatial properties to complement his list of official titles during his reign as Hitler's deputy. As Minister President of Prussia, he had an official residence at Leipziger Platz in Berlin refurbished at the state's expense, in addition to a hunting lodge in Rominten Heath in East Prussia (formerly owned by Kaiser Wilhelm II), a summer house on the German island of Sylt and an alpine house in the Obersalzberg at Berchtesgaden. He also claimed ownership of two castles belonging to his late godfather.

His profligacy was not confined to his private realm. He employed more than 100 staff in his private office at the Air Ministry, when a fraction of that number would have sufficed. In March 1943 Goebbels enjoyed a rare moment of *Schadenfreude* on overhearing Hitler berating Goering for allowing himself to be influenced by his subordinates, who were forbidden from bringing the Reichsmarschall bad news. Ironically, Hitler would be served in the same way when he was no longer capable of accepting unpalatable facts without flying into a rage.

But for all his bravado and bluster the Fat Man was often prey to self-pity and whined that he had to play second fiddle to Hitler.

'Just try playing the crown prince for 12 whole years,' he later complained to Nuremberg court psychologist Gustave Gilbert, 'always devoted to the king, even though disagreeing with many of his political actions, but incapable of doing anything about it and having to make the best of the situation.'

Anti-war Stance

In the early days of 'the struggle', while the Nazis were preoccupied with internal squabbling, Hitler had considered Goering his only true friend, but their relationship became strained when it became clear that Goering did not share his Führer's hunger for war.

In September 1938, while the Nazi leadership waited for the Czech government's response to their ultimatum regarding the surrender of the Sudetenland, Goering almost came to blows with von Ribbentrop. Although it was Hitler's bluff that had brought Germany to the brink of war before it was ready, Goering did not have the courage to confront his Führer and so he exchanged insults with the Foreign Minister, whom he called 'Germany's Principal Parrot'. By this time, Hitler had the measure of his deputy, who was revealing his reluctance to go to war. The previous year Goering had drafted the Munich agreement giving the Czechs a last-minute reprieve, which infuriated Hitler who was straining at the leash. Denied his war, Hitler's affection for Goering cooled considerably.

For this reason, Hitler kept Goering in the dark regarding his plans for the invasion of Czechoslovakia on 15 March 1939.

'I was furious because the whole thing had been decided over my head,' Goering later remarked.

Goering could foresee that the invasion would discredit the British prime minister, Neville Chamberlain, who would doubtless be succeeded by a bullish and far more formidable adversary, Winston Churchill. But Hitler lacked similar foresight.

Later that summer, while Hitler pored over plans for the invasion of Poland, Goering was actively pursuing every possible opportunity to secure peace through backdoor diplomatic channels, being acutely aware that the Luftwaffe was ill-prepared for a protracted campaign. His own sources confirmed that Britain and France would mobilize if Poland was invaded, though Hitler was adamant that the Allies were bluffing. After the opening salvos had been fired and German troops were pouring across the Polish border, Hitler appointed Goering his successor and the Fat Man's fate was sealed.

In the summer of 1940 Goering was horrified to learn that Hitler had set his sights on Russia. A war on two fronts would be military suicide, he argued, but Hitler was adamant that Stalin's recent purges of the army leadership had left the Soviet Union effectively defenceless and demoralized. It would only take one kick at the front door, as he put it, to bring the whole rotten structure down.

Goering later remarked to one of his generals:

'It is economically wrong, politically wrong and militarily wrong. But von Ribbentrop wanted it and Goebbels wanted it and they persuaded the Führer to want it too. I protested until I was blue in the face, but they would not listen. Now I wash my hands of the entire matter – the entire war. Do what you can. I can't worry any more about what is going to happen.'

Nepotism

Goering revelled in his image as an unprincipled rogue, but his gruff exterior and vindictive cruelty concealed a fatal weakness. He was by nature indolent, credulous and cavalier to the extent that he would frequently delegate a vital task to a subordinate and neglect to supervise its completion. Arguably his most serious misjudgement was in entrusting vital air production in January 1939 to Ernst Udet, a former comrade from the Richthofen squadron. Udet proved to be incapable of organizing and supervising manufacturing on such a scale and his failings went undetected until it was too late. He shot himself on 27 November 1941, blaming Goering for his fate. Hitler appointed Albert Speer to succeed Udet as Armaments Minister and within three years Speer had tripled the production of aircraft from 11,000 to 38,000, but with a fuel shortage the planes were invariably grounded.

Goering was in the habit of appointing old comrades to key positions within his ministry regardless of their qualifications, but he risked incurring Hitler's displeasure when he appointed Erhard Milch State Secretary in the Air Ministry, for Milch was partly Jewish. However, Milch was only one of more than 70 senior officers in the German army who had Jewish ancestry. Their origins had been deliberately overlooked by Hitler when he countersigned their commissions.

At the height of the war the Luftwaffe lacked long-range bombers, a deficiency any conscientious commander-in-chief would have made it his business to know, but Goering was preoccupied with the acquisition of titles, medals and the trappings of power. The distraction cost him his standing with Hitler and arguably contributed to the ultimate fall of the thousand-year Reich. Thereafter the role of the Luftwaffe was determined by Hitler alone. Goering received his orders directly from Hitler and was expected to carry them out without question. He was not even informed of Hitler's intention to declare war on the United States following the Japanese attack on Pearl Harbor on 7 December 1941.

Wealth Acquisition

As the war turned against Germany, Goering retreated from reality and the public eye. Unable to face the inevitable, or to influence the outcome, he spent more time at Carinhall among his looted treasures, hosting ever more extravagant parties while leaving a nation to face its fate.

At Carinhall, he indulged his passions and his fantasies and he had the means to do so.

German industry bribed him with ostentatious presents, including a yacht said to have cost 1.5 million Reichsmarks, and he also received monetary gifts.

The largest of these was a substantial payment from Philipp Reemstma, who bribed Goering to drop corruption charges against his tobacco company and to end a hate campaign in the Nazi press. In addition, Goering agreed to stop a proposed SA boycott of Reemstma's cigarettes, which were then in direct competition with the SA's own brand 'Sturm' – and all for the trifling sum of 3 million marks.

Of course, the payments were never declared as such but

went through Goering's accounts as 'donations' to German forests and the state theatre, of which he had control as Prussia's Minister of the Interior.

Goering was not as dim-witted as Goebbels had claimed. He may have played the buffoon in his custom-made Ruritanian uniforms, but he was sufficiently astute to acquire significant holdings in essential industries, specifically iron ore deposits, lignite mines, steel mills, gravel pits, coal mines and shipping lines. His vanity, however, prevented him from pursuing his business interests on the quiet. Every asset bore his name as if proudly trumpeting his involvement. He also raked in hundreds of thousands of Reichsmarks annually as a company director, though he rarely put in an appearance at the board meetings of Daimler-Benz or BMW. He was also not slow in seizing the assets of émigré industrialists such as Fritz Thyssen, who fled the country abandoning his steel mills, shares and other holdings to the avaricious Reichsmarschall.

Reputation in Tatters

Hitler was willing to overlook Goering's personal failings until they affected his judgement, for it was Goering who had been largely responsible for convincing wealthy and influential industrialists as well as the major financial institutions to back the Party when it was in desperate need of campaign funds. It was Goering too who had secured the support of the army and who had persuaded President von Hindenburg's son Oscar to allay his father's fears regarding the appointment of Hitler as chancellor, back in January 1933.

It was for these reasons that Hitler felt he owed Goering

his support, in acknowledgement of which he named the Fat Man his successor. But when the Reichsmarschall failed to prevent the British from evacuating the remnants of their beaten army at Dunkirk in May 1940, his swaggering boasts lost him much credibility with both Hitler and the High Command. Goering's failure to win the Battle of Britain and to prevent Berlin from being bombed, despite his boast to the contrary, left his reputation in tatters. But the final nail in the Fat Man's coffin was his failure to make good his promise to supply the besieged German Sixth Army at Stalingrad from the air which, on 2 February 1943, brought about the humiliating surrender to the Soviet forces of 91,000 frozen, starving, exhausted and demoralized German

THE FINAL NAIL IN THE FAT MAN'S COFFIN WAS HIS FAILURE TO MAKE GOOD HIS PROMISE TO SUPPLY THE GERMAN SIXTH ARMY AT STALINGRAD

troops, together with a significant number of their Axis allies. Goering assumed that he could repeat the feat of supplying encircled troops as he had done at Demyansk the previous year, but then there had been comparatively few Soviet troops and anti-aircraft guns in the area to pose a serious threat to the German planes.

The campaign in Russia taxed the Luftwaffe to its limits and depleted its resources to such an extent that Goering was no longer able to boast of German air supremacy in the west. The Nazi leadership was forced to face the fact that it had seriously underestimated the size of the Soviet forces, as well as Russia's capacity to rearm and restock its army from factories beyond the range of German bombers. No sooner had the Germans repelled one counter-attack than another would be launched. There appeared to be no end to the number of men Stalin was prepared to sacrifice to repel the fascist invader. Hitler had launched the invasion of Soviet Russia in the unrealistic belief that the Germans 'only had to unleash another mass armoured assault as they had in May 1940 to demoralize and rout Soviet forces fatally weakend after Stalin's purges of the officer corps'. Having learned to his cost that it was not so, he could not afford to admit to such a catastrophic misjudgement, and so laid all the blame on Goering, who despite his bluster had no stomach to stand up to Hitler. As Goering himself later confessed: 'Whenever I meet him, my heart drops into my pants.'

A Hierarchy Doomed to Fail

The truth is that the Nazi hierarchy was fated to fail. Hitler was no military genius, whatever his sycophantic subordinates might have told him. He was, however, a master of bluff and brinkmanship, abilities which secured Germany spectacular coups in the years preceding the war as the Reich gobbled up the French-occupied Rhineland, the German-speaking Sudetenland, pro-Nazi Austria and defenceless Czechoslovakia, all without firing a shot. Then reckless opportunism, speed, surprise and relentless momentum procured a swift and stunning victory over France and the Low Countries in May 1940, utilizing General Guderian's 'blitzkrieg' stratagem.

Following this astonishing run of luck, the myth of Hitler's infallibility, his interminable interference and his insistence that he knew better than his commanders undermined all efforts to capitalize on the advantages won by the Wehrmacht. Hitler had blamed Goering for losing the Battle of Britain but if the Luftwaffe had won air superiority and the Royal

Air Force airfields had been put out of action, Operation Sealion, the invasion of Britain, would have failed because Hitler had not made adequate preparations. There was no armada to carry the troops across the Channel, only a hastily assembled fleet of barges that the RAF reduced to matchwood while Goering's fabled Luftwaffe were engaged elsewhere.

Goering's distractions and childlike weakness for titles, uniforms and the symbols of power compounded the problem.

As early as May 1941, the Reichsmarschall sought to legitimize his looting of Europe's museums and art galleries by issuing a decree designating all 'cultural assets' as the property of the Reich. At first he contented himself with stealing everything of value from the Jews, offering worthless receipts or nominal amounts under the veiled threat of transportation to a concentration camp. Then emboldened by his success he strutted into the finest museums and art galleries, simply pointed his fat finger at whatever he fancied and ordered it to be shipped back to Germany. An estimated 26,000 railway wagons packed with looted treasure were transported from France alone on his orders.

As far as art was concerned Goering was a gourmand, not a gourmet. His taste was governed by the value of the pieces and paintings he acquired rather than their aesthetic qualities. He hung priceless masterpieces by the Dutch masters in tiers from floor to ceiling in Carinhall as if they were rare postage stamps or coins in a child's collection. His other residences were cluttered with sculptures, statues, tapestries, antiques and weapons in an ostentatious display of wealth and privilege, but a conspicuous lack of discrimination. Like their owner, it was all show and spectacle.

But his insatiable appetite for art and luxury cost him

dearly. While Goering was scouring the galleries and museums of occupied Europe, Martin Bormann was doing all he could to erode the Fat Man's standing with Hitler. Goering's absence was alluded to at critical moments when his presence was required and Bormann would recount Goering's earlier blunders to compound the felony, like the loyal functionary that he was. Goering became the butt of crude jokes among the Reich Chancellery staff and he was publicly cold-shouldered on more than one occasion when he offered Hitler his hand. But as Goebbels commented in June 1944, Hitler could not afford to replace the Reichsmarschall as it would reflect badly on the regime and his own judgement.

Final Days

The German public too were becoming more contemptuous of Goering's idle boasts, following the defeat at Stalingrad. While the ordinary German soldiers suffered privation and defeat at the front and their families cowered in bomb shelters from relentless day and night Allied air raids, Goering strutted in the newsreels in his Ruritanian uniforms with a supercilious grin on his face – like 'a vacantly smiling mollusc', to quote the Nuremberg prison warden. Even his own Luftwaffe was offended after he foolishly sent each squadron a gramophone recording of a recent speech condemning them as cowards.

More significantly, Goering was still so in the thrall of his Führer that he refused to put Germany's jet fighter, the Messerschmitt 262, into combat in June 1944 when there was still a chance to turn the tide of the air war because Hitler had determined that it should be reserved as a bomber. When Goering finally plucked up the courage to act on his own initiative on 23 April 1945, he did so only after satisfying himself that Hitler was physically and mentally incapacitated.

It must have been a pathetic scene: the debauched deputy making a pretence of loyalty while assessing his Führer's capacity to govern. Both men were mentally and physically enfeebled by drugs and facing the imminent destruction they had brought upon themselves – one driven by the desire to save his skin at all costs and the other kept alive only by his hatred for those he blamed for robbing him of an empire he had once boasted would last a thousand years.

After Goering fled Berlin for Berchtesgaden, he sent Hitler a radio-telegram, which Bormann intercepted, asking for confirmation that his Führer was still alive and able to issue orders. Goering ended by stating that if he did not receive a response by that evening he would assume 'overall leadership of the Reich' and would then act 'for the good of the people and Fatherland'. Bormann presented Goering's concern as an ultimatum and a treasonable act of betrayal. He got the response he hoped for – a venomous rage in which Hitler denounced his deputy and demanded his immediate arrest. But it was a hollow victory, for Bormann would not live to see Hitler's orders executed. He was killed in a failed breakout from the bunker after Hitler had expelled Goering from the Party in a last act of vindictive spite before blowing his own brains out.

Even after the war, as a prisoner in Nuremberg, Goering continued to exercise influence over some of the defendants – von Ribbentrop, Streicher and Sauckel in particular – in an attempt to prolong the illusion that he retained a semblance of his former authority, but Speer, Frank and Schacht remained stubbornly independent. It was only after they informed the prison authorities of Goering's attempts to coach them in their defence that the former Reichsmarschall was physically isolated from his co-defendants when their presence was not required in court.

On trial for his crimes at Nuremberg in 1946, a substantially slimmed-down Goering stunned the court by claiming: 'The people just needed someone to love and the Führer was often too distant from the masses. So they latched on to me.' Evidently he was deluded to the end.

Rudolf Hess (26 April 1894–17 August 1987)

'Hess was slightly off balance for as long as I can recall.'

Hermann Goering, 1946

The only member of the Nazi hierarchy whom nobody conspired against and who was not perceived as a threat by the other members of Hitler's inner circle was Deputy Führer Rudolf Hess. Goebbels damned him with faint praise by referring to him as 'a dear chap', while von Ribbentrop's adviser Reinhard Spitzy may have been nearer the truth when he dismissed the Deputy Führer as a 'likeable nutcase'.

Others viewed him as a slavishly devoted sidekick and something of an embarrassment. Even Hitler treated him as a faithful pet, referring to Hess in private as '*mein Hesserl*'. Hitler had appointed Hess his deputy in 1933 even though he knew that Hess was incapable of leadership, but he was a safe bet. Hess was without ambition and Hitler could rely on his unwavering loyalty.

'I just hope that Hess never has to replace me,' he told Goering in a rare moment of levity. 'I don't know who I'd be more sorry for, Hess or the Party.'

When Goering expressed his dissatisfaction with the deputy leader, Hitler reassured him that he could appoint his own successor, in the event that he became Führer.

It was common knowledge among the leadership that Hess 'couldn't string a sentence together', in the words of Party speaker Hermann Esser, and that he was not endowed with common sense. It was Hess who had been partly to blame for the failure of the Munich Putsch by allowing two prize hostages to escape. Incredibly he had left the two Bavarian ministers unguarded and trusted that they would honour their word not to attempt to escape!

But Hitler felt he owed Hess much for introducing him to his former teacher, Professor Karl Haushofer of Munich University, who came up with the concept of *Lebensraum* (living space) and discussed various geopolitical theories while the pair were serving a nominal sentence in Landsberg prison for the failed revolt.

Hess acted as Hitler's private secretary during their incarceration, but he did more than record the Führer's thoughts; he acted as his editor, formulating coherent arguments from Hitler's rambling monologues. But Hess's intensity proved too wearing even for Hitler, who complained bitterly of his deputy's intrusive presence. He eventually banned him from joining him at the Berghof for lunch after Hess insisted on bringing his own prepared vegetarian meals.

Flight to Britain

It is common to paint Rudolf Hess as a clown whose fanciful beliefs led him to ask for a package of soil from each region in the Reich to be sprinkled under his son's cot as a form of pagan baptism – a request characteristically rebuffed by Goebbels, who offered to send a paving slab from Berlin. He is also seen as someone whose 'natural sense of decency and honour', as Hitler's old adversary Otto Strasser put it, would have been outraged by some of the policies Hitler proposed. Before his ill-fated flight to Britain and his real or feigned insanity, Hess had been an active and willing signatory to the iniquitous Nuremberg Laws which deprived German Jews of their human rights and he had willingly consented to the euthanasia programme under which the mentally and physically disabled were murdered and a false death certificate sent to their families.

Hitler publicly disowned Hess and stripped him of his title after the Deputy Führer's ill-fated solo flight to Britain in May 1941, but there remains the possibility that Hess was authorized by Hitler to fly to Britain. If so, it would have been to avoid a war on two fronts while there was still time to come to an agreement with the British before Hitler launched Operation Barbarossa, his invasion of Russia, in June 1941.

Hitler's manservant, Heinz Linge, recalled that on the morning of Hess's flight he had knocked on the Führer's bedroom door at 9.30 to inform him that Hess's adjutant had arrived with an urgent message. To Linge's surprise Hitler was already dressed and shaved, although he had given orders that he was not to be woken until noon, his customary hour.

'It flashed through my mind that he had already known. There was no other explanation for his already being dressed, shaved and waiting in his bedroom. In all the years, I had never seen that before . . . I noticed that he only showed surprise, anger or bewilderment in the presence of others . . . I could not help thinking about the four-hour meeting that Hitler and Hess had had on the Obersalzberg several days before the flight. The two of them had not had such a long meeting since before the war.'

It seems likely that Hess embarked on his ill-conceived mission as a last desperate attempt to avert the inevitable and humiliating defeat he foresaw for Germany if Hitler was permitted to pursue a war on two fronts. But as idiosyncratic as his actions might appear in retrospect, he may have believed that he had no choice as Bormann had effectively isolated the devoted disciple from his beloved Führer.

But even if Hess had remained in Germany after May 1940, it is certain that he would eventually have been sidelined by the man destined to replace him, Martin Bormann. It says much about Hess' credulity that in July 1933 he appointed the man who anyone else could see was determined to succeed him.

Martin Bormann (17 June 1900–2 May 1945)

'Every educated person is a future enemy.'

Martin Bormann

Brutality

Hitler cared little that his acolytes were continually at each other's throats or that they loathed his most trusted aide, Martin Bormann. He conceded that Bormann was 'a brute', but he admitted that he found him invaluable and knew that he could rely on him to deal with the wearisome details of administration.

Hitler is recorded as saying:

'I know that Bormann is brutal. But there is sense in everything he does and I can absolutely rely on my orders being carried out by Bormann immediately and in spite of all obstacles. Bormann's proposals are so precisely worked out that I have only to say yes or no. With him I deal in ten minutes with a pile of documents for which with another man I should need hours. If I say to him, remind me about such and such a matter in half a year's time, I can be sure that he will really do so.'

Speer said of Bormann, 'Even among so many ruthless men, he stood out by his brutality and coarseness,' while Goering simply expressed his wish that 'the Brown eminence' should 'rot in hell'.

Bormann rationalized his lack of principles by alluding to the laws of the jungle. 'Unfortunately this earth is not a fairyland,' he said, 'but a struggle for life, perfectly natural and therefore extremely harsh.'

Ironically, he was not initially perceived as a threat by his colleagues. As Speer observed:

'Most of the powerful men under Hitler watched each other jealously like pretenders to the throne . . . but none of them recognized a threat in the shape of trusty Bormann. He had succeeded in representing himself as insignificant.'

Bormann was not endowed with above average intelligence, but he was sly, calculating, cunning and inhumanly patient.

He worked his way up the Nazi hierarchy by the back way, accumulating incriminating evidence in his secret files while taking no active part in the murders of political rivals, so there was nothing that could later be traced back to his office. But his information on the sexual indiscretions of the SA leadership in particular would prove damning and decisive when Hitler was assessing the threat posed by Röhm in the weeks leading up to the Night of the Long Knives.

Bormann preferred the shadows, avoiding publicity at every opportunity. He was notoriously camera-shy and refused all requests for interviews with the press, believing that the less people knew about him the better.

Himmler kept his distance as the two circled each other, neither daring to strike at the risk of being stabbed in the back by the other. But in January 1937 Himmler thought it prudent to ingratiate himself with Bormann, knowing that Bormann had the power to assign foreign slave workers to the forced labour programme, which was to prove a useful and profitable 'resource' for the SS. Consequently Himmler conferred the honorary title of SS general on Bormann, whose vanity was satisfied. Thereafter he and Himmler made an effort to accommodate each other whenever a potential disagreement arose.

Goebbels too affected an air of cordiality out of self-preservation until 1937, when Bormann became convinced that the film *The Broken Jug* (starring Emil Jannings as a blustering village magistrate), which had been sanctioned by Goebbels, was a thinly veiled attempt to ridicule him.

Seven years later Bormann showed that he was not a man to forgive or forget. After Goebbels had drawn up a 40-page memo outlining his strategy for a last-minute alliance with

Soviet Russia, he was horrified to learn that Bormann had locked it away in his office safe so that Hitler would never read it.

LIKE ANY OBSESSIVELY DEVOTED SERVANT, BORMANN STUDIED HIS MASTER ASSIDUOUSLY, ADOPTING HIS ATTITUDES AND EVEN HIS HABITS

Like any obsessively devoted servant, Bormann studied his master assiduously, adopting his attitudes and even his habits. He went to bed in the early hours when Hitler retired and rose at noon to trot behind the Führer, pen in hand and white index cards in his top pocket, ready to note down every utterance as if they were the words of a prophet. He affected a virulent hatred for the Jews when he saw that it met with Hitler's approval (and conveniently that of the odious Frau Bormann) and he embraced a strict vegetarian diet in the Führer's presence, though in private he gorged himself on pork chops whenever he could be sure that he would not be seen. Bormann, a devout Lutheran, even denounced Christianity to please Hitler and became an outspoken advocate of the neo-pagan cult of National Socialism.

On 17 June 1941 Bormann issued a secret directive to all regional Gauleiters instructing them to do all in their power to weaken the influence of the Church. If necessary, false charges were to be brought against the clergy in order to discredit them.

'National Socialist and Christian conceptions are incompatible,' he wrote. 'The Christian churches build upon men's ignorance; by contrast, National Socialism rests upon scientific foundations . . . But never again must the churches be allowed any influence over the leadership of the people. This must be broken totally and forever.'

Ménage à Trois

Bormann enjoyed a peculiar relationship with his wife Gerda, for whom National Socialism had become a religion. In accordance with its edicts she bore her husband ten children and encouraged him to father more with his mistress, Manja Behrens, whom she invited to live in the family home.

A letter he wrote to her in January 1944 elaborates on their uncommon arrangement. Bormann addresses his wife as 'sweet mummy girl', then continues:

> 'You know that in the beginning there was nothing between M [Manja] and me. I only found her attractive because she put me off . . . I arranged it so that I met her again many times and then I took her in spite of her protests. You know my willpower, against which M was of course no match . . . I feel doubly and happily married. O dearest, you cannot imagine how happy I feel with the two of you!'

His wife's reply was addressed to 'my sweetest and dearest daddy'.

'I love M so much that I simply cannot be angry with you. The children also love her very much. You must make sure that M has a child one year and I the next.'

Gerda then urged her husband to 'enlighten' his mistress as to the merits of National Socialism so that she would come to renounce her Christian beliefs, specifically the one relating to marriage. She might then find it easier to accept that a man could have more than one wife.

The following month Gerda shared her recent reflections

on the matter, adding: 'Experience teaches us that these relationships are often very happy. The husband, freed from the minor daily irritations, would have a better temperament.'

Bormann was not, however, burdened with 'minor daily irritations', nor did he require his wife's approval to abuse his subordinates. He took every opportunity to force himself on the hapless young stenographers who waited patiently to take dictation at the Berghof and was frequently seen ushering them into a side room, to the disgust of Eva Braun who warned her friends.

Bormann's duplicitous personality was reflected in his choice of official residence. To ensure that he was never more than a few metres from his master, Bormann purchased a former children's sanatorium a short walk from the Berghof and spent a small fortune converting the two-storey villa into a palatial residence. The plain brown exterior hid an opulent interior fitted with modern appliances, handmade carpets and marble bathrooms, all paid for by the state. Few guests were invited to share its comforts and those who were so privileged knew better than to gossip and risk making an enemy of Bormann.

Rumour-monger

The Reichsleiter had few friends, but preferred it that way. He ruled over a small army of subordinates, officials and administrative staff, all of whom would be kept at a distance and could be relied upon to stay silent about what they witnessed. None would risk incurring his displeasure. It was well known that he had soured the long-standing friendship between Hitler and Heinrich Hoffmann, the Führer's official photographer, for no reason other than to assert his malign influence over the Führer. The fewer confidants Hitler had, the better for Bormann. Every candid admission overheard during idle conversation was something he could use to his advantage.

When Hoffmann learned of a farmer who had been sentenced to two months in prison for withholding more milk than his ration allowed, he joked that he would receive a far stiffer sentence if anyone found out that he had done the same. Bormann informed Hitler of this and also hinted that Hoffmann had been infected with paratyphoid, transmitted by unpasteurized milk from the cows on his small farm. Hoffmann was subsequently barred from all future meetings with Hitler, but Bormann was not satisfied.

After Hoffmann had obtained a clean bill of health Hitler still refused to meet him, having been told by Bormann that the certificate issued to his former friend had in fact been issued to Hoffmann's son and that Hoffmann Senior was still carrying the fatal bug.

Bormann inched his way to the top of the heap by spreading rumours and innuendo about officials he did not like or whose lifestyles did not meet with his approval. Baldur von Schirach, leader of the Hitler Youth, suddenly found himself cold-shouldered by Hitler after Bormann let it be known that Schirach's sexual proclivities were well known and that rumours of his 'effeminate white bedroom' were rife among the press rooms and familiar to the Party's enemies.

Schirach narrowly avoided a scandal by relinquishing his role as leader of the Hitler Youth to Artur Axmann and 'volunteering' for the army. On his return he was appointed governor of Austria and Gauleiter (regional Nazi Party leader) of Vienna, but he soon disgraced himself in the eyes of his Führer by allowing his wife to raise the taboo subject of Jewish persecution.

Henriette von Schirach had recently witnessed a round-up of Jewish women in Amsterdam and was appalled at the brutality meted out to them, so on their next visit to the Berghof, Hitler's alpine retreat, she asked Hitler what he knew of these deportations. All colour drained from the Führer's face and he screamed at her that she was sentimental and had to learn to hate. The couple were asked to leave immediately and were never again invited to tea at the Berghof.

Bormann made a fortune for Hitler by initiating schemes such as the Adolf Hitler Endowment Fund of German Industry, to which wealthy industrialists 'donated' vast sums in the belief that they would be buying influence with the Party leadership. He was also said to have dreamed up the idea of siphoning off a percentage from the sale of postage stamps bearing the Führer's likeness, which raked in 75 million marks during his 12 years in power, although Heinrich Hoffmann asserted that the scheme had been his idea. And it was Bormann who introduced compulsory accident insurance for all members of the Party, which swelled the organization's coffers. By such seemingly minor incremental steps, Bormann gained the advantage and made up for his lack of intelligence and education.

Private Secretary

Bormann's unnatural patience and dogged persistence paid off in April 1943 when Hitler appointed him his private secretary, a post which ensured that no one was permitted access to the Führer without Bormann's approval. He also determined which messages Hitler should see and which should be withheld until they would bring the response Bormann desired. But his greatest coup was in obtaining the authority to issue orders on the Führer's behalf, some of which were no more than casual remarks which Bormann transcribed into directives.

Shortly after his promotion, Alfred Rosenberg noted:

'Hess had obviously got on the Führer's nerves, and so Bormann took care of the queries and orders. Here is where he began to make himself indispensable. If, during our dinner conversation, some incident was mentioned, Bormann would pull out his notebook and make an entry. Or else, if the Führer expressed displeasure over some remark, some measure, some film, Bormann would make a note. If something seemed unclear, Bormann would get up and leave the room, but return almost immediately after having given orders to his office staff to investigate forthwith, and to telephone, wire or teletype.'

The Committee of Three

By the spring of 1943 Bormann's continual intervention was impeding access to the Führer and delaying decision-making at a critical time. There were also rumours – well founded as it happened – that Bormann was attempting to consolidate his position by forming an alliance with Field Marshal Wilhelm Keitel and Hans Lammers, Ministerial Councillor and Hitler's chief legal adviser. 'The Committee of Three', as it was referred to at the time, would unite the Party, state and military who would then be in a position to relieve the Führer of some of his most burdensome duties. But Goering, Goebbels and Speer managed to veto the plan by making their opposition clear to Keitel and Lammers.

When he learned of Bormann's intentions, Goebbels confided to Speer that the time had come to remove the Reichsleiter before it was too late. Hitler was then conducting the war from the Wolf's Lair, his heavily fortified headquarters near Rastenburg in Poland and had made it known that he did not want to be distracted by 'trivial' administrative issues. Goebbels told Speer:

'It cannot carry on like this any longer. We are here in Berlin. Hitler doesn't hear what we have to say about the situation; I have no influence with him; I cannot explain even the most urgent measures relating to my own area to him. Everything goes through Bormann. Hitler must be talked into coming to Berlin more often. Domestic policy has totally slipped through his fingers; it is now being conducted by Bormann and he is able to give Hitler the impression that he is always on top of everything. Bormann is driven only by ambition; he is dogmatic and a danger to any sensible development. His influence must be limited immediately! We have not only a Staff crisis, but strictly speaking, a leadership crisis.'

It was Speer who offered to put their case to Goering, as the Reichsmarschall had the authority to issue decrees without Hitler's approval. However, Goering was not on speaking terms with his colleague in the Ministry of Propaganda after the latter had ordered the closure of Goering's favourite restaurant on the grounds of wartime economy.

When Speer arrived at Goering's home on the Obersalzberg he found his host dressed in a green silk dressing gown on which he had pinned a large ruby brooch. He was made up like an ageing brothel madam with garish red nail polish and rouge on his cheeks. While Speer outlined the plan, Goering fidgeted with a handful of precious stones as if in a drug-fuelled daze, but appeared to understand what was being proposed. He was evidently gratified to have been taken into their confidence, for by this time he was unsure that Hitler still had faith in him.

> **GOERING WAS MADE UP LIKE AN AGEING BROTHEL MADAM WITH GARISH RED NAIL POLISH AND ROUGE ON HIS CHEEKS**

A week later Speer returned, this time with Goebbels. According to Goebbels, Goering had expressed enthusiasm for their plan to force 'the pact of three out of the way' and 'shift the power to a new council of ministers'. But they were as distrustful of their potential allies as they were of each other, and so agreed not to confide the ultimate aim to those they hoped to win over to their side, only to canvass their support in the hope of isolating Bormann and re-establishing a direct line to Hitler.

Goebbels recorded his satisfaction in his diary. 'I believe that even the Führer will be very happy about this.'

But within weeks Goering was out of favour again after Hitler blamed him for failing to defend German cities against the intensifying Allied air raids, specifically the combined attack on Hamburg which continued unopposed day and night for a week, leaving half the city reduced to rubble and killing 40,000 civilians, and so the proposed 'coup' did not take place.

But in the end, even Bormann left Hitler to his fate. After assuring his Führer that he would remain at his side to the bitter end, the faithful servant sneaked out under cover of darkness in an effort to save his skin.

For more than 50 years following the Fall of the Third Reich, Bormann became an elusive, almost mythical figure with reported sightings in South America and North Africa. He had been sentenced to death *in absentia* at Nuremberg for his part in the enslavement and murder of countless foreign workers and prisoners of war whom he had signed over to the SS and for authorizing the execution of captured Allied airmen. He was also charged with having instructed district governors (Gauleiters) to report any suspected cases of lenient treatment so that he could punish those who had neglected their duties.

But all that time his body had remained under rubble a few hundred metres from the bunker. His remains were unearthed in 1972, but they were not positively identified until a DNA match with a surviving relative could be made in 1998.

Albert Speer (19 March 1905–1 September 1981)

While Albert Speer served as Hitler's architect he was spared the malicious sniping that characterized life among the leadership, but as soon as he accepted the role of Armaments Minister, he found himself thrust into the snake pit.

Prior to his appointment Speer had enjoyed an informal relationship with Hitler, who relished every opportunity to pore over plans of ambitious new construction projects with a fellow artist, including the extensive rebuilding of Berlin along classical Roman imperial lines. Hitler looked to Speer to fulfil his unrealized dreams of monumental buildings that were conceived to last a thousand years and thereafter leave imposing ruins for the world to marvel at.

But when Speer succeeded the previous incumbent, Fritz Todt, on 8 February 1942, following Todt's death in a mysterious air crash, he found his relationship with Hitler and the other Nazi leaders had cooled considerably. It was strictly business from then on, with a bitter spat over departmental authority fought out in a series of tersely worded memos.

On one occasion Speer complained to Himmler that the SS guards at Mauthausen were 'over generous' with regards to their use of resources – both human and materials – and that they could be far more productive if they were prepared to devise a 'more sensible deployment of available manpower in the concentration camps' in order to meet the 'current demand for war materials'.

Being an efficient technocrat, Speer assigned one of his subordinates to make routine 'on-the-spot inspections' of all camps, which prompted the SS officer in charge of supplying forced labour, Obergruppenführer Oswald Pohl, to complain that any deficiency was to be laid at Speer's door, as the SS were only complying with his direct orders.

It was a squabble that might have aroused enmity between management and factory supervisors in a commercial business, only this spat was played out between the perpetrators of state-sanctioned genocide whose labour force was worked, starved and beaten to death. Of the 10,000 inmates of Sachsenhausen concentration camp who were drafted into the *Arbeitskommando Speer* to quarry the stone needed for the Führer's new buildings, only 200 survived.

Corruption was endemic among those in power, for there was no democratic authority to call them to account. Inevitably, their self-serving philosophy filtered down to every branch of the administration and those civilian businesses that served them. Manufacturers stubbornly resisted turning over their factories to the production of armaments and munitions until October 1943, when Speer threatened them with 'the Himmler treatment' if they did not comply. Even if they were fiercely loyal Party members and supported the war, they were primarily looking to enrich themselves if they could get away with it and many did, bribing Party officials with 'gifts' for unspecified favours.

For this reason, both regional and local officials were quick to seize on the chance to snipe at Speer when he was temporarily incapacitated with a serious illness in January 1944. The carping was so vicious and widespread that on his recovery Speer offered to resign but Hitler wouldn't hear of it.

According to Speer, he and Himmler were continually vying with each other for power, with Himmler ordering the arrest of members of Speer's workforce on false charges so that they could be reassigned to SS factories. As a consequence, productivity suffered under Speer, which occupied and infuriated him more than the ill-treatment of the prisoners, especially as he would be held to account for the fall in productivity. Speer was also frustrated by Himmler's squandering of resources (mainly manpower) on eccentric and impractical projects, after various cranks had managed to convince the Reichsführer that they would improve productivity and win the war.

Speer's recollections are, however, to be read with caution as he used his various memoirs to support his claim to having been 'naive' with regards to the appalling conditions suffered by the prisoners assigned to his armaments factories and forced labour camps.

Even as the Allies encroached on the Reich in the last months of the war, Himmler persisted in his efforts to undermine Speer's authority. At the root of his enmity was the belief that Speer was ill-suited and unqualified to fulfil his responsibilities as Armaments Minister. The fact that the short-sighted, physically enfeebled Himmler was equally unqualified to head the elite SS did not restrain him from attempting to exercise his authority over other departments, even though in doing so he was undermining the war effort.

Alfred Rosenberg, Nazi 'Philosopher' (12 January 1893–16 October 1946)

Alfred Rosenberg's enemies mocked him for having 'a second-rate mind', so it is perhaps fitting that he was accused of writing the second most vilified book in literary history, *The Myth of the 20th Century*. In common with *Mein Kampf*, very few readers actually managed to read it through to the end.

Rosenberg's infamous and fallacious diatribe was deemed required reading by the Nazi leadership, but on the witness stand at Nuremberg every one of the defendants denied having read it. In private Hitler had dismissed it as 'illogical rubbish' and 'trash that no one can understand', while Goebbels poured scorn on both the book and its author by dismissing it as 'an ideological belch'.

It was Goebbels who nicknamed the would-be Nazi 'philosopher' *Beinahe* ('Almost') Rosenberg because he 'almost managed to become a scholar, a journalist, a politician, but only almost'.

Rosenberg was aware of his own shortcomings as a politician, admitting in his memoirs that he prevaricated when it came to making important decisions and found it difficult to assert himself. But it was precisely for his lack of leadership qualities that Hitler appointed Rosenberg acting leader of the *Grossdeutsche Volksgemeinschaft* (a front for the disbanded NSDAP) when he was sentenced for his part in the Munich Putsch in March 1924. Hitler knew that there were men such as Gregor Strasser who wanted to seize the reins as soon as their leader was out of the way and he needed to be sure that the man he chose would not pose a serious threat to his rivals while he was absent.

Rosenberg freely admitted: 'Hitler values me a great deal, but he does not like me.'

Rosenberg thought of himself as an intellectual and imagined he was highly regarded, while his opponents within the Party saw him as nothing more than a pompous and conceited snob who made no effort to disguise his disdain for the working class members. They resented his affected air of superiority and found themselves continually having to remind him that the Party had been founded by workers for workers and that it was not a platform for part-time politicians who wanted to make a name for themselves.

Racial Theorist

But Hitler needed someone to justify the Party's unfounded anti-Semitic sentiments with something resembling a reasoned argument and Rosenberg appeared well qualified as he had received a decent education, although he had evidently failed to distinguish the difference between fact and fiction. It was Rosenberg who perpetuated the myth that all races were intellectually and physically different and that the white 'Nordic' or Aryan race was superior in every respect. Rosenberg contended that interracial breeding had led to the contamination and weakening of the Aryan people, who must purge themselves of tainted blood. He argued that only by 'purifying their race of impure elements' would they attain their destined role as the Master Race.

Rosenberg's reasoning was fatally undermined by his reliance on an infamous forgery, *The Protocols of the Elders of Zion* (a scurrilous piece of anti-Semitic propaganda which was used as 'documentary proof' that the Jews were part of a global conspiracy). He also drew on the fanciful and absurd theories of Richard Walther Darré, whose book *Blood and Soil* advanced the idea that the soil of Germany was fertilized by the blood of those who had been buried in it and that by consuming the produce of the land that blood would strengthen their descendants.

Robert H. Jackson, American prosecutor at the Nuremberg war crimes trial, was surely alluding to Rosenberg's illogical, ill-informed and illiterate hotchpotch of ideas when he accused the Nazi leadership of 'intellectual bankruptcy'. It was indicative of Rosenberg's lack of moral fibre that he back-pedalled when challenged to substantiate his inflammatory racial slurs, unable to provide any proof for his irrational assumptions.

'I didn't say that the Jews are inferior. I didn't even maintain that they are a race. I merely saw that the mixture of different cultures doesn't work.'

A Monarch Without Land

Hitler was hard pressed to find an official post for Rosenberg. He had coveted the role of Minister of Foreign Affairs, but Hitler gave this position to von Ribbentrop. In its place, he found himself playing host to foreign visitors under the grand but meaningless title 'Deputy to the Führer of the National Socialist Party for the Entire Spiritual and Ideological Training of the Party'. And they said Hitler had no sense of humour!

But Rosenberg was to find a significant role in June 1940 and one that was to lead him to the gallows at Nuremberg – that of head of the *Einsatzstab Reichsleiter Rosenberg*, the official arm of the regime entrusted with the theft of art treasures from the occupied countries. Within six months, Rosenberg estimated the value of the loot taken from France alone to be one billion Reichsmarks. And it was only the beginning. In total over 10,000 priceless paintings were shipped from France and the Low Countries to Germany.

Then in April 1941 Rosenberg was promoted to Reichsminister for the Eastern Occupied Territories, in anticipation of a successful campaign in Russia. He imagined himself lording it over the Slavs, who would be forced into slavery to provide for their German masters. Southern Russia would be turned over to the production of food for the conquerors, with the local population being fed only as much as was required to maintain their efficiency. However, they would be

ROSENBERG ESTIMATED THE VALUE OF THE LOOT TAKEN FROM FRANCE TO BE ONE BILLION REICHSMARKS. AND IT WAS ONLY THE BEGINNING

allowed to practise their religion in order to pacify them, for they were regarded as little more than savages who worshipped pagan idols.

The Germans also imagined that the tedium and anguish of being enslaved would be alleviated by piped music such as that which kept workers at their machines in the Soviet factories.

But the humane treatment ended there, for the Germans would permit their slaves to communicate with each other only through sign language. Their breeding would be controlled by forced abortions and their movements restricted to the designated areas of the villages where they lived and worked like medieval serfs serving their German overseers.

Education was to be denied them as they would have no use for it.

Rosenberg's vision of living the life of a modern pharaoh was short-lived, because his directives were disregarded by Himmler, Sauckel and the other Reich Commissars who circumvented his authority and ignored his protests. Sauckel argued that he required men for the various forced labour projects inside Germany, including the excavation of the V1 and V2 rocket sites at Peenemünde, while Himmler demanded slave labour for the SS-run factories and concentration camps. Goering too exercised his priority as overseer of the Eastern economy, leaving Rosenberg a 'monarch without land or subjects', as Goebbels labelled him.

Hitler's 'philosopher' finally came to realize the futility of all his efforts in late 1944. It was only then that he understood how much he was despised by the leadership. No one even acknowledged receipt of his resignation.

Joachim von Ribbentrop
(30 April 1893–16 October 1946)

Herr Brickendrop

If there was one thing the Nazi leadership could agree upon it was whom to hate. Officially it was the Jews, but in private their scorn was centred on one man – Ulrich Friedrich Wilhelm Joachim von Ribbentrop.

The Nazi Foreign Minister was an easy target for ridicule as he was patently unsuitable for the position to which he had been appointed. Hitler had assumed that the business connections acquired by von Ribbentrop while he had been employed as a champagne salesman might prove useful in negotiations.

The Führer, whose experience of the world had been limited to the battlefields of France and Belgium during the First World War, was also impressed by the fact that von Ribbentrop had travelled abroad, specifically to North America where he had cultivated a brief relationship with Joseph Kennedy. However, he had reckoned without von Ribbentrop's stupefying insensitivity and ignorance of diplomatic protocol.

When greeting King George VI, von Ribbentrop nearly poked the royal eye out with a whiplash Nazi salute (a faux pas that earned him the nickname 'Brickendrop'), while his imperious, arrogant and bullying manner alienated both his staff and foreign dignitaries. He delighted in having his English butler attend him with phone in hand while he took his morning bath. When anyone rang, they were told to wait until he had emerged and wrapped himself in a towel, by which time most callers had rung off.

The British took an instant dislike to his affected English accent and his theatrical manners, but most of all they frowned upon his blatant attempts to be accepted into society and into the gentlemen's clubs, all of whom refused to support his application for membership. Worse still, he was so woefully ignorant of foreign affairs that when he was arrested at the end of the war he was carrying a personal letter addressed to 'Vincent' Churchill.

The Nazis should have known better than to entrust foreign policy to someone as lamentably incompetent and inept as von Ribbentrop. If they had devoted a fraction of the resources they squandered on tracing the Aryan ancestry of suspect citizens to investigating von Ribbentrop, they would have discovered that his potential value to them had been assessed 30 years before by one of his teachers, who regarded the youth as 'the most stupid boy in his class'.

Conceited

It's true, he was not the sharpest of men, but he recognized an opportunity when he saw one and was probably one of the few Nazis to make a fortune during the years of hyperinflation. He bribed customs officials in the French-occupied Rhineland to turn a blind eye to his exporting of French wines and spirits from the duty-free zone into Germany. In gratitude, his customers gave him tips that helped him make a killing on the currency market while his country slipped into the Great Depression.

He was shamelessly conceited too, acquiring the aristocratic 'von' in 1926 after begging a senile relative to adopt him. That episode in particular made him a figure of fun in the eyes of Goebbels, who mocked him behind his back, laughing that he had 'bought his name, he married his money and he swindled his way into office'. The latter comment was a reference to the fact that von Ribbentrop had initiated his own diplomatic missions in 1934 after having been overlooked for the post of Foreign Minister, in the hope of proving himself useful to the Führer. Hitler was easily impressed and after dubbing him 'the second Bismarck' he appointed him ambassador to London two years later.

It is likely that he was given the post on the recommendation of his rival Constantin von Neurath, the Foreign Minister, who wanted to keep von Ribbentrop out of the way for fear that he would meddle in foreign affairs, for which he was evidently unsuited. Von Ribbentrop suspected that had been the case and delayed his departure as long as he could, after which he found innumerable excuses for returning to Germany, which earned him the nickname 'the wandering Aryan'.

But to everyone's surprise von Ribbentrop rewarded Hitler's faith in him the following year by overseeing the signing of the Anglo-German naval agreement, which secured the Allies' permission to rebuild the German navy while restricting the size of ships and armaments. Von Ribbentrop was also instrumental in reviving the Anti-Comintern Pact, which secured the strategic support of Nazi Germany's Axis allies.

However, it was only a matter of time before von Ribbentrop exceeded himself by trying to deceive Hitler. In 1938 he was called to account for the excessive expenditure incurred in running his 'Ribbentrop Bureau', a private office he had set up in 1932 to cultivate business contacts and spy on his competitors. Nazi Party treasurer Franz Schwarz had discovered that von Ribbentrop was employing a staff of 350 and paying them out of Party funds. When Hitler heard about this, he demanded to know how many people his minister was employing. Von Ribbentrop told him it was only 150, at which Hitler was said to have exploded with rage.

'What? You dare to lie to me?' he shouted.

That same day the Ribbentrop Bureau was closed down, 200 employees were dismissed and the remaining 150 were reassigned to the Foreign Office, to the consternation of their new colleagues who resented the influx of men who were only qualified to click their heels and bark 'Heil Hitler'.

By this time von Ribbentrop had replaced von Neurath as Foreign Minister and further resentment threatened to bring the Foreign Office to a grinding halt after the new incumbent introduced a compulsory uniform, an army-style ranking system and daily inspections for all staff, male and female. Every morning the entire staff were lined up in the courtyard and their uniforms were subjected to

VON RIBBENTROP BECAME A FREQUENT GUEST OF THE JEWISH HOSTESSES OF THE BERLIN AND FRANKFURT SALOONS

von Ribbentrop's hypercritical eye before he issued his orders for the day.

It has been said that he only succeeded von Neurath as Foreign Minister because Hitler could rely on him to do as he was told. But in truth, Hitler owed von Ribbentrop a senior posting for having engineered his succession to the chancellorship in 1933 by setting up a crucial meeting with von Papen in the home of the influential banker Franz von Schröder, the banker who had 'loaned' the National Socialists the millions they needed to secure the required number of votes in the election campaign.

Von Neurath had only contempt for his successor, saying:

'That commoner has always peddled his wares to the highest bidder. May God have mercy on the Reich!' Years later, while awaiting trial at Nuremberg, von Neurath informed his interrogator that no official in the Nazi administration was held in lower esteem than von Ribbentrop, adding: 'He actually did more harm than good with his stupid meddling.'

Fake Briton

The best that could be said for von Ribbentrop was that he did not have a reputation as a rabid anti-Semite, having once been in business with Jewish banker Herbert Gutmann to distribute French wines and spirits, but overnight he found that adopting a violent anti-Jewish attitude brought Hitler's approval. It was also a profitable stance to take and allowed the former champagne salesman to buy his ex-employer's business for a fraction of its true value. The wine importer Sichel and Company of Mainz was valued at 4.5 million marks when von Ribbentrop acquired it for a mere 100,000 marks.

He made a healthy profit from his partnerships with Jewish bankers and soon became a wealthy man and a frequent guest of Madame Rothschild and other Jewish hostesses of the Berlin and Frankfurt salons. There he took an active part in their English drawing room comedies staged for the delight of their guests and was commended for his cut-glass English accent, which prompted Robert Ley, the Nazi Labour Front Leader, to joke that von Ribbentrop now spoke German with an English accent. Of course, once he became a prominent Nazi, von Ribbentrop was *persona non grata* in the Berlin and Frankfurt salons, but by then he had no need of his former friends.

Appointing von Ribbentrop Foreign Minister was a fatal error of judgement on Hitler's part, for von Ribbentrop offended practically everyone that he came in contact with, ensuring that the British establishment looked unfavourably on Germany's approaches regarding an alliance against Soviet Russia in the years prior to the Nazi–Soviet pact. Had Hitler appointed a competent man, he might have succeeded in influencing that faction of the British establishment, the appeasers, who were then urging the government to make further concessions to Nazi Germany.

But von Ribbentrop was too conceited to play the part of the diplomat. The counterfeit aristocrat would keep exclusive Savile Row tailors waiting all morning before sending them away with a request to come back the next day. Consequently, they informed their blue-blooded clients that von Ribbentrop was not a gentleman.

He was dubbed 'Ribbensnob' by his British critics and although he went to considerable lengths to ingratiate himself into high society, befriending the likes of King Edward VIII and his American mistress Mrs Simpson, he did so in the mistaken belief that the nobility influenced British foreign policy.

It was not only his singular lack of tact but also his appalling taste that offended British sensibilities. *Life* magazine reported that von Ribbentrop's first act on arriving at the German Embassy in Carlton House Terrace was to rip out the quaint traditional features to enable him to host receptions and dinner parties for 200 guests. Furthermore, he had the insensitivity to impose charmless National Socialist décor throughout the period property. He had barely been in the country for a month before he was facing the wrath of the English Society for the Protection of National Monuments, who objected to the defacing of the 18th-century frescoes, ceilings and mantlepieces. His wife also found the natives less than friendly when she ordered the grass in front of the embassy to be dug up and replaced with a rock garden. British bureaucracy proved to be every bit as intractable as its German equivalent. The Commissioner for Parks and Lawns informed Frau von Ribbentrop that she would need to obtain approval for her plan from the other residents, which put an end to that particular venture.

The arrogant ambassador shrugged it all off as a mild nuisance, but he was stung when his eldest son Rudolf was refused entry to Eton, taking it as a personal insult. The boy was subsequently sent to Westminster School and during his holidays was often to be seen lounging on the front terrace of his parents' villa in Dahlem, Berlin reading a copy of *Mein Kampf*. This happened so frequently that journalists soon came to the conclusion that he had been deliberately posed there by his father for effect.

After war broke out, there was little for von Ribbentrop Senior to do but busy himself behind a desk when not playing host to representatives from Germany's Axis allies. Even they found him insufferably pompous, with Mussolini describing the Nazi diplomat as 'an imbecile'.

Heinrich Himmler
(7 October 1900–23 May 1945)

Early Years

Albert Speer had the measure of Heinrich Himmler, the physically unprepossessing and unlikely leader of the Gestapo and the SS, when he referred to him as 'a completely insignificant personality . . . half schoolmaster, half crackpot'. Others remarked on Himmler's excessive servility, his obsessive attention to detail (he even kept a filing system to record the gifts he had been given) and his neurotic compulsion to account for every mark that his office spent.

His sense of duty and desire to please his superiors was unhindered by principles or scruples, which he did not possess. The German journalist Guido Knopp suggested that he was a man who personified the 'minor virtues' of order and obedience, a sense of duty, respect for authority, hard work and thrift. These had been drummed into him by his father, a pedantic provincial schoolmaster who found fault in everything his children did and was said to behave obsequiously to his superiors and to be overbearing to his pupils.

The second of three sons, Himmler was named after his godfather, Prince Heinrich of the Bavarian court, whom his father had taught and against whom he was measured and invariably found inferior.

As a child he was shy, solitary and introverted as well as being encumbered with poor eyesight and chronic stomach ailments, which excused him from sports and healthy outdoor activities and gave his father further cause for disappointment. Instead, he absorbed himself in stamp collecting and learning to play the piano, hoping to earn parental approval through his musical prowess, but he abandoned the instrument in frustration after ten years of fruitless effort.

The young Heinrich was given a journal to keep even during his school holidays and his daily entries were corrected by his overbearing father. During term time, Heinrich was ordered to spy on his fellow pupils by his father, who was the principal, an activity which he was to continue as head of the SS, taking an interest in his men's private lives which bordered on the voyeuristic.

He was too young to volunteer for the army when war was declared in 1914, but three years later he enlisted and spent the final year of the war as a clerk. When Germany surrendered he enrolled in Munich Technical High School as an agricultural student and then went on to study chemistry and biology at the university. After graduating he worked as a poultry farmer and fertilizer salesman but soon found himself caught up in the extreme nationalist movement and joined a right-wing paramilitary organization. There he came into contact with SA leader Ernst Röhm and found a position as an office assistant to Gregor Strasser, Hitler's bitter rival in the early years of the Nazi Party. Unlike Hitler, Strasser took the socialist part of the Party's name in all seriousness.

Gregor's brother recalled his impressions of the young Himmler, describing him as 'keen' and looking 'like a half-starved shrew'. Himmler would spend all day touring the farms and villages scavenging for weapons and succeeded in building a formidable arsenal that would be used to fight their communist rivals.

Expansion of the SS

Never one to miss an opportunity for advancement, Himmler began to feed Hitler information on Strasser that he would subsequently use to oust his rival. As a reward Himmler was appointed second-in-command of the SS, Hitler's elite bodyguard, which at the time numbered fewer than 300 men. It was a promotion which confounded Hitler's advisers, but the SS was then subordinate to the SA and the role of second-in-command was not seen as being of great significance or conferring any authority.

Himmler was by nature a rather weak and spineless individual who was acutely aware of his physical inadequacies and puny physique, which would have disqualified him from serving in the SS. To compensate for his deficiencies and lack of character he sought unquestioning obedience from his subordinates, whom he ordered to commit acts of cruelty that he could not have carried out himself, mistaking their compliance for respect. In turn, his enemies interpreted his callous indifference as demonic cruelty. He had no compunction however, in turning on a former comrade as he did the night he ordered the murder of Gregor Strasser, his former superior, during the Röhm purge in July 1934. With Röhm and his lieutenants out of the way, the SA was fatally weakened and the way was clear for Himmler's ascent to prominence.

Himmler found an unlikely ally in Goering when the time came to stem the rise of the SA. The two men shared a loathing for Röhm, who was making unreasonable demands on Hitler for political influence within the Party. Goering wanted Röhm eliminated so that he could secure the deputy leadership for himself, while Himmler coveted the power Röhm wielded as leader of the Brownshirts.

When the bloodletting was over, Goering was promised the deputy leadership (though he was not appointed as such until Rudolf Hess disgraced himself by flying to England on his ill-conceived peace mission). Himmler, however, immediately capitalized on Röhm's death and the purging of his paramilitary organization by expanding the SS from 60,000 to a formidable force of 3 million and one that was independent of the Party and exempt from the laws governing the ordinary citizen.

Ironically, Himmler revealed his blatant disregard for both the law and the rights of the ordinary citizens who were at his mercy in a speech he gave to the Academy of German Law in October 1936. From that moment, the SS was effectively above the law and its leader was answerable to only one man – Adolf Hitler.

The previous November, Himmler had identified the four principles which he believed were fundamental to the SS creed. The first, he stated, was the recognition of the importance of the physical characteristics of the SS soldiers and the 'purity' of their Aryan blood, which should be 'uncontaminated'

THE PRINCIPLES FUNDAMENENTAL TO THE SS CREED HAD ALL BEEN DRUMMED AND BEATEN INTO THE YOUNG HIMMLER BY HIS FATHER

by Semitic 'impurities'. The second was their will to fight and their will to freedom (by which he meant their freedom to do as they saw fit, regardless of moral and legal constraints). The third principle was loyalty to the Führer and the honouring of their oath of devotion to the National Socialist *Weltanschauung* (world view). In this, the heart was to rule the head; in other words they were not to think but to act out of a sense of duty. The fourth and final principle was unquestioning obedience to their superiors. These were all principles that had been drummed and beaten into the young Himmler by his father. Now he had found a new father, one who was stern but approving of his 'faithful Heinrich' – Hitler.

Curiously, Goebbels considered these questionable attributes to be admirable, commending Himmler for his industry and honesty and describing the former chicken farmer as 'cultured' and 'good-natured', which reveals more about the Propaganda Minister's twisted sense of values than it does about Himmler.

Projects and Schemes

Unlike Goebbels, the Reichsführer SS did not profit financially from his position. He lived rent-free in a large but unprepossessing house in Dahlem, Berlin and appeared content with his salary of 24,000 Reichsmarks, although he lavished millions of marks on his private projects. The most lavish of these was the refurbishing of Wewelsburg Castle in Westphalia, which would serve both as a training school for his SS elite and as the perfect setting for the quasi-magical practices that Himmler hoped would give his black order of Teutonic Knights an aura of mystical invincibility. But his intense interest in alternative therapies, the esoteric and the occult were all on a very superficial level. He had no deep learning or experience of these matters. He was a fantasist who seized on every outlandish theory that supported the belief in the superiority of the Aryan race.

His sponsoring of fruitless expeditions in search of religious artefacts and his funding of fanciful projects such as the aborted tunnel to the Earth's core in 1941 squandered precious resources. The latter saw millions of Reichsmarks being spent on the excavation of a 16-kilometre tunnel at a secret location in Hungary, down which Himmler planned to descend in a cable car to make contact with a mythical race.

But Himmler's most iniquitous scheme was the establishment of the *Lebensborn* maternity homes, where eligible German girls would make themselves available for impregnation by

SS men with the aim of producing a Master Race of pure Aryan supermen. Both single and married men were expected to participate in the programme, which had been envisaged as a countermeasure to the edicts of the Catholic Church. Encouraging extramarital relationships was Himmler's way of undermining Catholicism, which he had rejected as a young man and now wanted to see ripped up 'root and branch'. Christianity was to be replaced by the neo-pagan cult of National Socialism; the cross was to be substituted by the swastika, the Bible by *Mein Kampf* and Jesus by Germany's own messiah, Adolf Hitler.

Himmler and Margarete

Himmler's puritanical zeal had led him to take a vow of chastity prior to his marriage in July 1928 to Margarete Boden, a woman seven years his senior, and a vow of fidelity thereafter, but all this was soon forgotten. Once he realized that his uniform and authority held a certain attraction for many women he exploited it to indulge in an affair with his secretary, Hedwig Potthast, with whom he fathered two illegitimate children. Himmler set his mistress up in comfort in a specially built love nest in Berchtesgaden at a cost of 85,000 Reichsmarks, arranged by Martin Bormann.

The sexually inexperienced Himmler was attracted to his wife, a blond, blue-eyed divorcee, partly because she was a nurse and owned a share of a private health clinic which he hoped would support him, while her medical knowledge promised a cure for his chronic ailments. As a divorcee she held little hope of finding a husband and saw him as a way of escape from the 'impossible' Jewish doctors whom she despised but had to work with. Her misanthropic nature and assertion that women were the weaker sex fed his fantasy of being a strong protector and helped him overcome his earlier fear of inadequacy.

Their letters reveal an infantile coyness, in stark contrast to the public image of callous indifference Himmler projected.

'You must know that you have a man you can call yours, who is deeply grateful to you for your love and whose every free thought that the struggle permits him, is of you – and who loves and honours you as the sweetest, purest thing he has.

'I hope that everybody is nice to you, that nothing gets on your nerves, and that you do not have to wrinkle your brow. I stroke your dear forehead and kiss your dear mouth.

'Your Heini.'

She saw little future for him in the Party and tried to persuade him to devote his life to making their dream of a small farm a reality. She resented the time he was spending with Hitler.

'Why are you going to a Hitler rally, you surely know what he's going to say?' she wrote.

'If only you did not have to go around with the Boss any more. He takes up so much time.

'It would really be nice if you were not a member of the movement. Leave that old Party.'

For all her National Socialist zeal, Margarete Himmler saw nothing hypocritical or unpatriotic in spending up to 1,300 marks a month (the equivalent of £16,000/$20,000 today) on 'little luxuries' for herself and her three children when ordinary citizens were restricted to getting by on as little as 50 marks a month.

Weird Correspondence

In 1933 the Himmlers adopted Gerhard von der Ahe, the five-year-old son of a murdered SA man, but Himmler did not regard him as the son he had always wished for and would beat him with a riding crop. The boy was sent away to a National Socialist school but was expelled for failing to achieve the required results and Marga refused to accept him back.

Hitler Youth leader Baldur von Schirach had the impression that Himmler was 'henpecked' by his domineering wife, while others of her acquaintance described her as being a provincial narrow-minded type who would have had little understanding of her husband's role in the regime. However, Margarete was fiercely proud of her husband's status in the Party and frequently found herself reminding her neighbours who she was married to. On one occasion she was being chauffeur-driven in the Himmler family car, which had the number plate SS2, when it was passed by another car. She immediately ordered her driver to overtake the impertinent locals so that she could remonstrate with them.

But the most bizarre revelation to emerge from the recent discovery of Himmler's private journal and letters is the weird nature of their intimate correspondence.

In one letter she wrote: 'I am so fortunate I have such a bad husband who loves his bad wife . . . as she loves him.'

To which he replied: 'The revenge – it will be fun. I am nothing but revenge forever. My black soul thinks about impossible things.'

Their mutual hatred for the Jews bound them together, a hatred which was compounded when Margarete was forced by financial circumstances to sell the health clinic that she part-owned to a Jewish physician. Her husband was sympathetic.

'Poor Lovey,' he wrote, 'you have to deal with the miserable Jews because of money.'

Friends Sent to Their Deaths

In public, the Nazi leadership professed to be ardent National Socialists, but in private they did as they pleased. Goebbels and Goering owned palatial villas, while their wives flaunted their Paris fashions and cosmetics in defiance of their Führer, who had made his distaste for such luxuries well known. He gleefully told his female guests at the Berghof and at official functions that their make-up was made from animal fat. Only Frau Bormann and Margarete Himmler conformed to the drab rustic image that for Hitler epitomized the ideal German mother. They dressed in *Tracht* (heritage clothing) as dictated by the Reich Fashion Institute and braided their hair in a bun. Margarete's brother-in-law (Heinrich's elder brother) described her as a cold, emotionless woman who suffered with her nerves and was continually complaining. Her one redeeming feature, he said, was that she was 'an exemplary housewife'.

NINI, MARGARETE'S ONLY CLOSE FRIEND, WAS THE WIFE OF A MAN WHO CARRIED OUT SADISTIC MEDICAL EXPERIMENTS ON INMATES AT DACHAU

She invited the wives of senior SS officers for afternoon coffee every Wednesday but had little to say to any of them and was disliked by most of her guests, who felt obliged to attend.

Even so, they found excuses to avoid her after she attempted to tell them what to do and where they should stand during the 1938 Nuremberg rally.

One Nazi wife who made no effort to hide her loathing for Margarete was Lina Heydrich. She refused her husband's repeated entreaties to befriend Frau Himmler and even went so far as to organize rival tea parties to draw the other wives away from Margarete. At first she merely insulted the dowdy Marga, as she was known, by referring to her weight and appetite for fattening cakes, but in August 1936 things became extremely unpleasant after Lina learned that Himmler had tried to persuade Heydrich to divorce her. In fact, Himmler and Lina refused to speak to each other for the next six years, their feud thawing only weeks before Heydrich's assassination.

Margarete's only close friend appears to have been Karoline 'Nini' Rascher, the wife of Dr Sigmund Rascher who carried out sadistic medical experiments on inmates at Dachau. Himmler had no qualms regarding Rascher's conduct in the camp, but he was enraged to learn that the couple had lied to him about their 'miracle' children by maintaining that Nini had given birth to them even though she was 48 at the time and sterile.

In fact, the Raschers had stolen the babies from an orphanage and claimed them as their own to earn the Reichsführer's approval. On top of that, Rascher had also been accused of embezzlement.

One thing Himmler could not forgive was being made a fool of, so Dr Rascher was packed off to Dachau where he is believed to have been executed in April 1945. His wife was imprisoned at Ravensbrück and was murdered there.

Detached from Reality

Himmler was detached from reality to such a degree that when he witnessed a mass execution in August 1942 he fainted and subsequently suffered a fit of hysteria (an incident he described in his diary along with details of his extramarital affairs). In the same pages he described himself as a 'decent' man and a 'romantic fantasist', who kept his role in the murder of millions from his wife in the belief that it might upset her.

His thought processes were so impaired that they amounted to a psychosis, one which had him imagining that he would be redeeming himself by sending thousands of balloons to children scheduled for extermination in Auschwitz.

His surviving letters and postcards home to his family were informal and familiar, with casual references to his 'work' and visits to concentration camps, and were signed off with his customary '*Dein Heini*' ('Your Heini') or '*Euer Pappi*' ('Your Daddy') when writing to his wife Margarete, whom he addressed as 'Dear Mummy' or 'My Dear Sweetheart'. However, when she learned of her husband's three-year affair with his secretary Hedwig Potthast in 1941, and the fact that Hedwig had given birth to two children, Frau Himmler was said to be deeply hurt and not entirely convinced that it was his 'Aryan duty' to produce more offspring. Himmler's affair with Hedwig is believed to have continued until a couple of months before his suicide in May 1945.

Himmler may have struck many who met him as no more than another crank in the mould of the *völkisch* 'mystics' Guido von List and Lanz von Liebenfels, whose spurious racial theories had influenced Nazi ideology, but he was sufficiently astute to profit from his 'eccentric' ideas. A strict vegetarian, non-smoker and teetotaller, Himmler invested the enormous sums raised by SS membership subscriptions in purchasing all the mineral water springs and extraction plants in Germany, as well as fish-processing factories, herbal medicine producers and furniture factories producing items made only from natural wood. Even the arch cynic Albert Speer revised his assessment of Himmler towards the end of his life, crediting the 'insignificant little pedant' with a keen ear, the patience to consider all options before making a decision and a talent for choosing efficient and capable people to carry out his orders. But perhaps Himmler's most valuable characteristic, as far as Hitler was concerned, was that he never aspired to be Führer, only to serve his leader. In 1929 he told his wife: 'Believe me, if Hitler told me to shoot my mother – I would do it.'

The reward for his loyalty was another title. In 1939 Himmler became Reich Commissar for the Consolidation of German Nationhood, which gave him political control over the conquered territories and made his SS responsible for the 'security' of the concentration, extermination and forced labour camps.

Views on German Women

Himmler's peculiar opinions on marriage and the role of women in German society were evident in the scrupulously detailed reports he compiled in support of SS marriage applications. Every SS officer was required to seek the Reichsführer's permission to marry and had to abide by his decision.

Himmler would deny the application if the woman in question did not conform to his personal standards or image of the ideal Aryan mate. An officer identified only as 'B' in the official SS records was refused permission to marry because his fiancée looked like a 'painted doll', her generous use of make-up making her 'entirely unsuitable'. Another was given Himmler's approval provided he managed to convince his future wife to reduce the amount of lipstick she wore. Himmler's notes revealed that he considered cosmetics to be a weakness indulged in by women of 'lesser races' and the 'foolish German women' who want to look like American film stars.

'Anyone who gets herself up like a half-caste . . . is denying her own good blood,' he wrote.

His own wife, the plain, dowdily-dressed Margarete Himmler disapproved of such immodesty and her husband had been raised with a similar attitude, although if he hadn't been he doubtless would have adopted that attitude to placate his wife.

Nor did he approve of women smoking in public, an aversion he shared with Hitler. Zealous Party members were instructed to snatch the cigarette from any woman seen smoking in public and warn her that such behaviour would not be tolerated. It is a wonder that so many women voted for a party that extolled such retrogressive and misogynistic attitudes.

But Himmler's intrusive meddling in the private lives of his men betrays a perverse personality. The secret SS files contain a note that one couple were advised to consider sterilization after Himmler had reviewed their family histories and believed their children to be at risk of 'hereditary impairment'. Anything short of Aryan perfection was considered unworthy of the Master Race, but strangely enough Hitler was the only member of the administration who would not have been able to offer documentary proof of his Aryan ancestry, possession of which was obligatory for every citizen of the Reich.

The racial origins of his men's choice of mate were of particular concern to Himmler, for the SS were conditioned to believe that they were the embodiment of Aryan attributes and heroic Nordic virtues. Himmler told them that they were the reincarnation of the Teutonic Knights who had kept the barbaric hordes at bay centuries before and were destined to do so again in the coming final battle with the Soviet invader. He believed himself to be the reincarnation of their leader, the first Saxon King Heinrich I (Henry the Fowler), although what convinced him that a brawny broadsword-wielding hero would be reborn as a short-sighted former poultry farmer with a puny physique and chronic stomach trouble is not recorded. He told his men that they were part of a soul group who had been reincarnated to share glorious victories and said they would meet yet again in the life to come, provided that they honoured their brotherhood and fulfilled its sacred blood vows through pitiless slaughter and self-sacrifice.

Only superior Nordic females could be considered worthy of such men. The shape of the skull, the colour of the eyes and the pigmentation of the skin were considered a rational basis for determining whether a potential partner would be good breeding stock for his SS supermen.

Obsession with Racial Origins

Ironically, the three men who were the most fanatical concerning the racial characteristics of those under their command would not have satisfied their own criteria. When the regime's leading 'racial hygienist' Max Gruber testified before the People's Court in Munich, he offered a less than flattering 'expert' assessment of Hitler.

> 'I saw Hitler from close to for the first time. Face and head bad racial type, crossbred. Low, receding forehead, ugly nose, wide cheekbones, small eyes, dark hair; facial expression not that of one in full self-control, but of one who suffers from insane excitement. Finally, an expression of complacent self-satisfaction.'

Gruber had characterized Hitler as East Slav and un-Nordic.

Racial origins as determined by the specious 'science' of phrenology were something that Himmler took a particular and unseemly interest in. It was an adolescent male fantasy that should have remained within the pages of Robert E. Howard's mythical tales of Conan the Barbarian, but then Nazism had been born of the fanciful mythology devised by German *völkisch* 'mystics' such as Lanz von Liebenfels and Guido von List. Their extreme nationalism and spurious racial theories had fed the racist fanatics of Hitler's generation with the belief that they were the descendants of an antediluvian race of superior beings, giants who had survived the destruction of the fabled islands of Atlantis and Lemuria. According to Liebenfels, List and others of that deluded brood, this race migrated to the shores of northern Europe where they mated with humans and begat the Aryans whose pure blood was now sullied by miscegenation.

Himmler saw himself as the custodian of this exalted lineage and was determined to reject any men who were said to be henpecked on the grounds that 'leaders who are incapable of leading a unit of two . . . are incapable of greater things'. But 'henpecked' is the very term Hitler Youth leader Baldur von Schirach chose when describing Himmler.

Character

Those who had occasion to be in Himmler's company for any length of time soon discovered that he was socially insecure, gauche and a poor conversationalist. Albert Krebs, Gauleiter of Hamburg, complained that Himmler was an 'almost intolerable' companion due to his (incessant) 'vacuous chatter', which he forced on his colleagues and acquaintances 'without interruption'.

Goebbels was being more than generous when he said that Himmler was a man who was 'not overly clever'. By all accounts he was not stupid, but he was, however, uncritical in the extreme and credulous to the point of naivety. At the end of the war, he believed he could negotiate the release of concentration camp inmates for a hefty ransom and with it secure safe passage for himself through the Russian lines. He arranged a meeting with a representative of the World Jewish Congress and greeted him with the words: 'Welcome to Germany. It is time you Jews and we National Socialists buried the hatchet.'

German historian Joachim Fest wryly observed that in a democratic society Himmler would have been relegated to the 'lunatic fringe' and limited to a field of activity that could involve publishing pamphlets or being involved in a sect. Only under a totalitarian regime could he have acquired the power that offered him the opportunity to put his ideas into practice. It is revealing that Himmler considered the indolent, uneducated and ill-informed Hitler an intellectual and a visionary to be worshipped and admired. Himmler's maxim, 'The Führer is never wrong', was repeated aloud at every opportunity.

Perhaps the most disturbing aspect of Himmler's character was his complete indifference to the suffering he caused his countless victims. He was not a sadist, like Mengele or Heydrich, nor was he a criminal who profited from the atrocities he authorized and approved, but he simply had no conception of the consequences of his indifference and inhumanity. He was incapable of compassion or of empathy, which made him the very embodiment of the *Untermenschen* he professed to despise.

Although Himmler cultivated the image of a leader who refused to profit from his position, he led the privileged life of a feudal lord. Having been named after his aristocratic godfather, Prinz Heinrich of Wittelsbach, he convinced himself that he was of noble birth. It therefore seemed appropriate that he should acquire the symbols of feudal power and a fitting setting in which to live out this fantasy.

Renovating Wewelsburg

He spent millions creating his own private Camelot by renovating the 12th-century castle at Wewelsburg near Paderborn in Westphalia, justifying the expense by claiming that the fortress had been the site of the legendary Battle of the Teutoburg Forest in AD 9, when the Germanic tribes had defeated three Roman legions. Himmler believed that the castle was destined to be the site of a final decisive battle against the invading hordes from the east and would thereafter be the symbol of Aryan superiority.

Victory had been foretold in the stars and so there was no reasoning with him, for Himmler was a firm believer in destiny and the occult science of astrology. The Ahnenerbe – a racial heritage research department founded by Himmler to find historical evidence to support specious Nazi theories of Aryan 'Nordic' ancestry and superiority – had discovered that the triangular fortress had been built on the intersection of several ley lines,

HIMMLER BELIEVED THAT WEWELSBURG CASTLE WAS DESTINED TO BE THE SITE OF THE FINAL DECISIVE BATTLE AGAINST INVADING HORDES FROM THE EAST

which meant that there was an uncommonly high concentration of natural etheric energies, making it ideal for the performance of ceremonial magic and other esoteric rituals. Himmler knew nothing of such practices, but he was convinced that the symbolic significance of the location, combined with the esoteric geometry of the castle and the natural energies it attracted, made it the perfect setting for SS initiation rites. The castle would be renovated and refurbished as an SS officers' training school, but in Himmler's mind it would be much more than an elite academy. It would be the 'spiritual centre' of the SS.

In 1941 plans were drawn up and models were made to show how the castle was intended to be incorporated into a much grander design which included an SS village with barracks, a hydroelectric dam and an airport. The North Tower of the castle would be at the base of a three-quarter circular wall topped with 18 smaller towers, its distinctive triangular-shaped foundations forming the shape of a spear. The shaft of the spear would be created by an access avenue and the tip of the spear would point north to 'the point of greatest darkness', in occult lore, as if to ward off the barbarians.

No expense was spared in renovating the castle. Himmler is believed to have spent a total of 15 million Reichsmarks on renovation and refurbishment between the summer of 1934, when work began, and 1943, when all non-essential construction in the Reich was prohibited. The human cost of renovating the castle was, however, incalculable. Over 1,200 forced labour workers from Sachsenhausen concentration camp were worked, beaten or starved to death during its reconstruction.

The moat was excavated and enlarged to match Himmler's image of a formidable stronghold, the floor of the North Tower was lowered and the interior was redecorated and furnished to accord with his idea of what a sacred site should look like. In Holland alone, 206,000 Reichsmarks were spent on paintings and *objets d'art*.

Gobelin tapestries hung from the freshly plastered walls and oak-panelled 'study' rooms, heavy brocade curtains framed every window and plush hand-woven carpets were laid on the stone floors. The finest craftsmen in Germany were commissioned to create everything the modern 'medieval' castle required from cutlery to candlesticks, all embossed with SS insignia. Carpenters were employed to carve the heavy oak furniture that had been designed to be in keeping with the imposing setting and a smithy was installed in the North Tower to fashion the ornate wrought ironwork that was used in the door handles and other decorative features.

In the Great Hall, 12 chairs were arranged around a circular table, each chair upholstered in pigskin embroidered with the occupant's coat of arms. Some have endeavoured to find occult significance in that number, citing the fact that there were 12 disciples and 12 signs of the zodiac, but it is more likely that it corresponds to the 12 departments of the SS, one chair being for each department head. Here the 12 senior SS officers would reputedly engage in guided visualization meditations aimed at contacting 'Hidden Masters' on the inner planes, to bring them victory and occult 'wisdom'.

But the only witness to what took place at these secret meetings was SS Brigadeführer Walter Schellenberg, Himmler's spymaster, who later recalled: 'Each member . . . had to devote himself to a ritual of spiritual exercises aimed mainly at mental concentration.'

On one occasion Schellenberg interrupted a psychic circle of SS officers attempting to read the mind of a suspect (General von Fritsch) being held in an adjacent room. In his memoirs Schellenberg wrote:

'[Himmler had] ordered them all to concentrate their minds on exerting a suggestive influence over the General that would induce him to tell the truth . . . to see these 12 SS leaders sitting in a circle, all sunk in deep and silent contemplation, was indeed a remarkable sight.'

The hall was decorated with the heraldic shields of the 12 SS chiefs, although few of the members were from titled families – Himmler included – so the Ahnenerbe was given the task of originating them.

Directly beneath the Great Hall was the circular crypt known as 'the realm of the dead', in which the ashes of fallen comrades were arranged on granite plinths around an eternal flame. In the event that the bodies of the fallen could not be recovered, their coats of arms would be burned instead and placed in a porcelain urn. Here too were collected the Death's Head rings given to each SS officer after three years' service, which had been designed by the man who came to be known as 'Himmler's Rasputin', Karl Maria Wiligut.

By war's end, there were said to be 9,000 rings stored in the tower, which Himmler had buried in a secret location the day he ordered the destruction of his Camelot. Only the North Tower remained.

Relics and Neo-paganism

Rumours that the notoriously squeamish Himmler held private séances with the severed heads of fallen SS officers only reveal how far the Reichsführer's interest in astrology, Aryan archaeology and sacred relics had captured the fevered imagination of some observers.

That said, Himmler once urged his men to mate in cemeteries where German heroes had been interred, in the belief that their disembodied spirits would be tempted to reincarnate in the wombs of their chosen partners.

Wewelsburg was to be the scene of SS marriages which assumed a neo-pagan character in keeping with Himmler's intention of supplanting Christianity with the National Socialist cult. The Reichsführer made a point of being present on these occasions so that he could give the couple his 'blessing'. Himmler also attempted to replace Easter and Christmas in the Nazi calendar by encouraging the celebration of the summer and winter solstices with candlelit processions and neo-pagan, nature-worshipping ceremonies at Wewelsburg and other SS centres.

Each room in Wewelsburg was named after an Aryan king or hero and furnished with armour, antique furniture and weaponry of the period, some of which had belonged to the king in question. These had been acquired in the belief that the relics possessed an inherent power that could be transferred to the present occupants. For the same reason, sacred artefacts were sought in far-flung locations by archaeologists and experts in the service of the Ahnenerbe.

Among the most sought after relics were the Holy Grail (the cup Jesus had drunk from at the Last Supper and which had caught his blood at the Crucifixion) and the legendary Spear of Destiny (which was said to have pierced his side to end his suffering on the cross).

The fact that these were holy Christian artefacts did not perturb Himmler, who had been persuaded that Jesus had been neither a Jew nor a Christian but an Aryan god after digesting the writings of the *völkisch* 'mystics' Lanz von Liebenfels and Guido von List. This specious revisionism was the precarious foundation on which the Nazis based their conflict with the Church, despite the fact that Hitler, Himmler and Goebbels were all Catholics.

There were ancient artefacts in the castle too, including a bronze Etruscan helmet and several spears that had been recovered by Aryan archaeologists, but not all of the art was of historical origin. Himmler commissioned numerous portraits that celebrated his status as leader of the SS as well as murals by Hans Lohbeck and sculptures by Anton Grauel, which included a figure that Himmler had admired in a magazine. He couldn't help interfering, even in artistic matters, and instructed Grauel to alter the features to conform with his image of the mythical Nordic ideal.

On the Art Trail

Himmler's image as a cost-conscious bureaucrat only applied to his private finances. As Reichsführer he had considerable funds at his disposal and spent them freely, but only after satisfying himself that the Reich was getting value for money. To this end, he employed SS Sturmbannführer Wilhelm Vahrenkamp from August 1942 onwards. Vahrenkamp's task was to scour private collections, galleries and museums for suitable paintings and other artefacts that could convey the impression that the Reichsführer was a man of culture and refinement. Himmler could have ordered the seizure of any priceless painting that caught his fancy, but he wanted to be seen to be a loyal servant of the state and to pay the market price. Laudable though this might have sounded, he frequently did so out of a fund known as *Sonderkonto R* and its subsidiary account the *Freundeskreis* ('economic enterprises'

HIMMLER PAID FOR PAINTINGS WITH THE PROFITS FROM THE DEATH CAMPS, INCLUDING MONEY FROM THE SALE OF GOLD TEETH

controlled by the SS), into which the profits from the death camps were deposited, including money from the sale of gold teeth torn out of the mouths of victims of the gas chambers.

Himmler also had a private train at his disposal, a large farm at Gmund, various temporary centres of operations, a palatial headquarters in Berlin and at least two well-appointed private residences – one at Dahlem for his wife and children and another at Obersalzberg for his mistress and the two children he had fathered with her. All were richly furnished with the trappings that came with power in Hitler's Reich.

By nature suspicious, Himmler feared that art experts might take advantage of his unlimited funds and his ignorance of the art world and be tempted to charge extortionate prices for mediocre pieces. Vahrenkamp was therefore not authorized to spend a pfennig without first obtaining his employer's consent.

Potential purchases would first be discussed with one or more experts that Himmler had on permanent call and whose opinion he trusted: men such as Professor Diebitsch, Hans Posse and the painter Wilhelm Peterson. Vahrenkamp knew a masterpiece when he saw one, but he took a commission and Himmler never underestimated the temptation that his representatives would be under to take an extra cut for themselves if they could hike up the price. He may also have been aware that Goering had the unenviable reputation among art dealers of being a sucker when it came to valuing works of art. On more than one occasion, the Fat Man had been duped into exchanging a priceless Impressionist from his collection for another with a far lower market value. In 1942 Dutch dealer and skilled art forger Han van Meegeren persuaded Goering to exchange 150 valuable paintings for a single picture supposedly by Vermeer. It was subsequently discovered to be a forgery.

Himmler visited the national gallery in Munich on several occasions and purchased work that appealed, but he also made a show of buying edifying portraits of Hitler and work by Hitler's favourite artists such as Arno Breker.

As Jonathan Petropoulos notes in his book *Art as Politics in the Third Reich*, there was a ritualistic element to Himmler's receiving and giving of gifts. His gift-giving was directed at two main categories of recipient; those in the Nazi leadership and those within the SS.

'In both cases Himmler sought to define a relationship through the giving of artworks.'

In the former case, these would be either expensive or of a personal nature, while in the latter situation cultural objects with symbolic significance such as candlestick holders and porcelain would be given to mark special occasions in the life of the recipient, to cement the bond of brotherhood between the SS leadership and its subordinates.

Reinhard Heydrich (7 March 1904–4 June 1942)

Jewish Ancestry Fears

The funeral of Reinhard Heydrich, 'Hitler's hangman', who had been mortally wounded in Prague by Czech patriots on 27 May 1942, was conducted with great solemnity as befitted a martyred Nazi 'hero'. But behind the scenes, the Nazi leadership breathed a collective sigh of relief for they knew that Heydrich had compiled secret files on them all – even the Führer – and that with his death the damning information in those files would never be used against them.

Heydrich too had lived with a secret during his brief and hateful life. The sadistic henchman to Reichsführer Himmler personified the archetypal Aryan male. Six feet tall, slim and in prime physical condition, he was an international fencing champion and a pilot. In fact, he could even have been described as a 20th-century Siegfried. But he was tortured by the belief that he was part Jewish, that his ancestry would be discovered and that he would be dishonourably discharged and publicly humiliated. It has been suggested that the existence of Heydrich's Jewish grandmother was no more than a malicious rumour spread by a disgruntled former pupil of his father, a music teacher. But whether true or not, the charge haunted Heydrich and doubtless contributed to his abnormal zeal in persecuting those he blamed for 'contaminating' his blood.

In 1930 his arrogant indifference and lack of scruples led

him to choose dismissal from the navy rather than marry a girl whom he had made pregnant. Soon after he married his fiancée, Lina von Osten, a fanatical Nazi who had evidently forgiven him for his 'unfortunate indiscretion', and was urged by her to join the SS.

Heydrich's contempt for the truth led him to lie to his prospective employer when interviewed for the post of Himmler's assistant. He told the Reichsführer that he had been an officer in naval intelligence and when asked to draw up a proposal for a new secret service (the SD) he drew on his familiarity with pulp detective novels to draw up a plan which impressed the credulous Himmler.

Nevertheless, the network of informers and electronic surveillance that Heydrich organized proved crucial in weeding out citizens and officials suspected of disloyalty to the Party, as well as gathering incriminating information and fabricating evidence that would be used to discredit senior army officers who had expressed opposition to Hitler's plans for war. In 1934 Heydrich's informants provided the basis for allegations against the SA, whom they had heard planning a coup to oust Hitler. A grateful Himmler responded by promoting Heydrich to head of the Gestapo and the SD. Three years later Werner von Blomberg and Werner von Fritsch were pressured into resigning their commissions after information manufactured by Heydrich was used against them.

Both Himmler and Hitler were aware of the questions concerning Heydrich's ancestry and they assured him that they were satisfied the rumours were unfounded, but Hitler later told Himmler that Heydrich could be 'extremely useful; for he would eternally be grateful to us that we had kept him and not expelled him and would obey blindly'.

Speculation regarding Heydrich's Jewish ancestry persisted long after he had received the Führer's official approval. On one occasion he had been on a drinking binge in Berlin with Admiral Canaris, Chief of Military Intelligence, when he insisted that his former superior should accompany him home for a final nightcap. As they entered the apartment, the intoxicated Heydrich was momentarily surprised to be faced with his own reflection. Whipping out his pistol he fired into the mirror, shattering the glass. There was a cruel twist to his lips as he mouthed what Canaris swore were the words 'filthy Jew!'

Secret Dossiers

Hitler's decision to 'pardon' Heydrich may have been influenced by his discovery that Heydrich possessed a dossier detailing the Führer's treatment for syphilis and, even more damning, proof that Hitler's Iron Cross had been awarded retroactively, long after the war had ended. It is unlikely that either allegation was true, but mere rumours pertaining to the existence of documents to that effect would have been extremely damaging to the dictator.

Heydrich was believed to possess thick files on Bormann and Himmler too, who was said to have been implicated in business dealings with Jews, a fact that would have undermined the Reichsführer's authority and would have cost him his position if it had been made public.

It was widely known that Heydrich would not be satisfied with playing second fiddle to Himmler for long, but was biding his time for the right moment to strike. Meanwhile he built a private fortune using blackmail and extortion, threatening to use the pages of *Das Schwarze Korps*, the official SS newspaper that he co-owned with Himmler, to reveal the names of businesses which had refused to appoint Nazi directors and individuals who had declined to contribute to Party collections.

By the summer of 1941 Heydrich had clawed his way to the top of the dunghill and was receiving credit both for his role in organizing the 'Final Solution' and for establishing the network of coded messages transmitted by a system of interlinked Enigma machines. This had helped secure early victories for the German war machine the previous year. His reward was to be his final posting as Reich Protector of Bohemia-Moravia, with Castle Hradčany in the Czech capital as his official residence and a mansion in the village of Paneské Břežany where he lived in splendour with his wife and three children.

Ironically, it was not the grenade thrown at his open car in Prague that killed him, but the fibres from the upholstery. Heydrich, the 'Butcher of Prague', died as he had always feared he would, from contaminated blood.

Hans Frank, Governor General of Poland (23 May 1900–16 October 1946)

Inquiry into Hitler's Origins

Hans Frank was Hitler's personal legal adviser and one of his most trusted lieutenants. As such he was given the power of life and death over the Polish population following the conquest of Poland in September 1939.

Frank joined the Deutsche Arbeiterpartei (DAP) or German Workers' Party (the forerunner of the NSDAP) in 1919, the year before Hitler became a member of 'that absurd little organization' and as a Brownshirt he took part in the Beer Hall Putsch, which made him one of 'the old guard' in Hitler's eyes.

He was elected to the Reichstag in 1930 and three years later he was appointed Bavarian Minister of Justice, a post which made him feel obligated to protest the murders of his former SA comrades during the Night of the Long Knives in July 1934 and of inmates at Dachau. Hitler responded with characteristic conceit, arguing that he had been the only law during the 'crisis' and therefore the killings were not unlawful.

Frank evidently didn't pursue the matter for shortly afterwards he was entrusted with a delicate and potentially highly damaging investigation into Hitler's ancestry.

Hitler said that his enemies 'must never find out who I am. They mustn't know where I come from, or my family background.' He feared that if rumours of his part-Jewish parentage were proven true, it would irreparably damage his standing in the Party and give his enemies the ammunition they needed to destroy him.

Frank's subsequent enquiries led him to conclude that it was likely that Hitler's father was half-Jewish. Hitler's paternal grandmother, Maria Anna Schicklgruber, had worked as a cook for a Jewish family who had paid her an undisclosed sum after she gave birth to an illegitimate child, the inference being that the father had been her employer's 19-year-old son. Frank discovered that the money had been paid on a regular basis until the child, Hitler's father, was 14 and that it had been paid to avoid a scandal. Maria Anna eventually married her second cousin, Johann Hiedler, when the boy was five and so he grew up as Alois Hiedler, which was later changed to Hitler so that he would qualify for a share of an inheritance bequeathed by an uncle.

A Hitler lookalike collects money for *Winterhilfe* (Winter Relief for the German People) – slogan: 'None shall starve or freeze.' People who failed to donate could find their names printed in local newspapers; others lost their jobs. Nazi officials were known to take a big cut.

Screen goddess Lida Baarova and actor Gustav Fröhlich chat to Joseph Goebbels at the Olympic Games in 1936. The Czech actress had a pre-war affair with Goebbels, which was ended by Hitler. Years later, Baarova insisted she had never been in love with the 'poison dwarf': 'Thanks to him I fell into the depths of Hell.'

When Hermann Goering and his wife, former actress Emmy Sonnemann, had a baby, little Edda, in 1938, he sent out 100,000 postcards showing the christening, perhaps in the hope of eliciting gifts but also to stifle rumours about his virility. It was said that the wound Goering sustained in the Munich Putsch had made him impotent.

Heinrich Himmler commemorates the anniversary of Henry the Fowler's death in AD 936 at Quedlinburg Abbey. Henry was the hero of Wagner's opera *Lohengrin*, and, despite his puny physique, Himmler believed himself to be the great warrior's reincarnation. The SS likened themselves to early Teutonic knights, but in Germany before the war chivalry was in short supply.

Nicknamed the 'Injection Master of the German Reich' and seen here in military uniform in Poland, Dr Theodor Morell was a shady gynaecologist who inveigled his way into Hitler's favour with quack remedies and a ready syringe. By 1945, Hitler was taking 28 different pills a day, supplemented by intravenous injections of methamphetamine. Hypochondriacs were Morell's bread and butter, and the neurotic Führer with his morbid fear of germs and other psychosomatic ailments proved a willing patient

Martin Bormann lived his life in the shadows, operating by stealth. He acted as Hitler's personal secretary and Nazi leaders had to go through him to get to the Führer. This gave the 'Brown Eminence' unimaginable power in Nazi Germany. Falling out of favour with Bormann meant losing everything. Bormann was a master of intrigue and political infighting, and because he deferred so brilliantly to his master, none of the Nazi leaders could depose him.

Hitler and Albert Speer (right) prepare for the 1937 Nuremberg Rally. Speer was everything Hitler wanted to be – cultured, urbane, socially adept and artistic. Hitler eventually appointed him Minister of Munitions. After the war, Speer made millions from his books, but he could never escape the Nazi taint, no matter how many excuses he came up with.

The very model of a humourless, fanatical Nazi, Theodor Eicke was commandant of Dachau, which he reorganized along barbaric lines as the template for all concentration camps. Eicke was a brutal, sadistic disciplinarian and is thought to have shot Ernst Röhm, leader of the SA, during the Night of the Long Knives in 1934. Eicke fought on the Eastern Front with the SS Death's Head division, and wherever he went atrocities were sure to follow. Few mourned his death in 1943 when his plane was shot down behind enemy lines near Kharkov.

Eva Braun and Adolf Hitler on the terrace of the Berghof with their dogs. Eva met Adolf when she was 17 and he was 40. Their 12-year relationship began when he invited her to the opera. At first, she was kept hidden from the public gaze because Nazi image-makers wanted to give people the impression that the Führer was 'married to Germany'. In the end their marriage was very brief: the honeymoon took place in Hitler's bunker and finished hours later in a suicide pact as the Russians rampaged across Berlin.

Sic transit Gloria mundi: American soldiers load some of the art collection looted by Hermann Goering, the self-proclaimed 'Renaissance Man', into a boxcar, near Berchtesgaden, in 1945.

Adolf Hitler gives his blessing to young members of the Hitler Youth, Berlin's last line of defence, some 10 days before committing suicide as the Russians closed in on the Reichstag.

The Chancellery in Berlin, 1945: American soldiers mock Hitler on the very balcony from which he delivered speeches.

Mass Murderer

Frank was a man of peculiar contradictions. His protests at the killings in Dachau and of Röhm and his SA comrades were not made out of compassion but out of concern for the legitimacy of the legal system. He wanted to counter accusations that the regime was using the courts to rubber-stamp its dirty work.

In October 1939, following the invasion of Poland, Hitler appointed Frank governor general, conferring on him the rank of Obergruppenführer SS, at which point Frank's murderous treatment of the civilian population began. While the Russians massacred Polish officers in their thousands at Katyn, their German allies arrested the country's intellectual elite and enslaved non-Jews in forced labour camps. Meanwhile Polish Jews were herded into ghettos in preparation for their transportation to the death camps of Treblinka, Sobibor, Chelmno, Majdanek, Belzec and Birkenau. Half a million were murdered in Belzec alone in a single year.

> **FOLLOWING THE INVASION OF POLAND, FRANK'S MURDEROUS TREATMENT OF THE CIVILIAN POPULATION BEGAN**

Frank would not be able to plead ignorance of their fate, having declared his intention to annihilate the Jews in a speech to Nazi officials in December 1941.

'We must annihilate the Jews wherever we find them and whenever it is possible.'

He also boasted that there were not enough trees in German-occupied Poland to provide the paper needed to list the civilians he had executed. Frank was subsequently accused of the murder of a million Polish non-Jews and of ordering the extermination of 3 million Polish Jews, whom he had transported to the six concentration camps under his jurisdiction.

Theft on a Grand Scale

But while Frank's principal role in their murder is well documented, his lesser crimes of theft on a grand scale are less well known. Following the capitulation of Poland he moved into the former royal palace of Wawel Castle in Kracow with his wife Brigitte and his four children. Although he was surrounded by looted art, which included pieces that had been set aside for Goering, Frank was not satisfied with second prize. He demanded the pick of Poland's treasures, including the nine Canaletto canvases that would take up the floor space in two palatial-sized rooms when Frank had them taken down in preparation for his escape in 1945. He also appropriated Leonardo da Vinci's *Lady with an Ermine*, Raphael's *Portrait of a Young Man* and Rembrandt's *Breaking Storm*, all of which are believed to have been earmarked for Hitler and Goering.

In common with many other leading Nazis, Frank had little knowledge of or interest in art and therefore recruited an expert to advise him on the acquisition of pieces that would give the impression that he was a man of culture and good taste. He was fortunate in recruiting SS officer Kajetan Mühlmann, an Austrian art historian who was to play a prominent role in Nazi art theft.

Mühlmann had been authorized by Goering to seize anything of value and have it parcelled up and packed off to Germany, as Poland was no longer considered worthy of

possessing priceless works of art. Frank showed his contempt
for Polish culture the day he moved into the former palace,
by tearing the embroidered silver eagles from the throne of
the Polish kings. He also considered the assets of the Polish
nobility to be his own personal property, including armour,
coins, porcelain, tapestries, manuscripts and antiques.

Frank's arrogance knew no limits. He considered himself
to be above the law – even Hitler's law – and thought he could
defraud his 'chief' by buying furs and jewellery for next to
nothing from Jews under duress and not declare them. While
their 'subjects' starved, the self-proclaimed 'King and Queen
of Poland' dined on delicacies imported illegally from Germany.
Wartime restrictions apparently did not apply to them.

Mühlmann later stated that he had sold valuable pictures
to the governor general for his private collection at his home
in Munich and that these had been purchased using sums
creamed off a 'great discretionary fund' that had been
earmarked for the acquisition of paintings for the Reich. In
addition, Frank had embezzled large sums from the
administration budget. He bought at least 100 paintings using
money set aside for official expenses, including a Bruegel
landscape and works by other Dutch Renaissance masters.

His unofficial acquisitions eventually came to the attention
of Himmler who ordered the SS to keep Frank under
surveillance in the hope of amassing enough evidence against
him, but when Himmler's report reached Hitler, the Führer
dismissed it out of hand. Frank was too efficient to lose. Better
to be certain of having a share of whatever Frank appropriated
than all of what a lesser thief might steal.

But in the summer of 1943 Frank was forced to share
power with Himmler, who had been appointed Minister of

the Interior for Poland, and Mühlmann refused to furnish any more paintings from the cache set aside for Goering – specifically Watteau's *Little Polish Girl*, which Frank had set his black heart upon.

Although Frank soon found a pair of more co-operative agents – Dr Werner Kudlich and Ernst de Palezieux – his power was on the wane. Himmler was asserting his authority over Frank, whom he regarded as nothing more than his political administrator.

Frank revealed another side to his peculiar personality when he was caught and put on trial at Nuremberg. Sweating profusely, he blamed Hitler for his fate and took refuge in religion, thanking God for bringing him before the 'world court'. Wringing his hands, he attempted to present himself as a victim, as 'an isolated, powerless man who had no influence on events'. He also claimed that he was in continual conflict with Himmler's representative, SS Obergruppenführer Krüger, who was theoretically subordinate to the governor general but who in practice frequently exercised his authority in order to anger him. Frank, in turn, initiated increasingly brutal acts of oppression in a futile attempt to prove himself worthy of Hitler's trust. On one occasion, he ordered a Jewish slave worker to be beaten for using his personal bath. The man's arms and legs were broken, so that he could be squeezed into the boot of a small car and then he was driven to a secluded spot in the forest and shot.

In the dock at Nuremberg he affected contrition and made a pathetic apology for the years of brutality he had inflicted on the Poles.

'A thousand years will pass,' he told the court, 'and still this guilt of Germany will not have been erased.'

He withdrew that statement soon after and went to the gallows with a smirk on his face.

Niklas Frank's Mission

Seventy-eight-year-old Niklas Frank carries a macabre souvenir with him when he visits German schools to lecture students on the crimes of the Third Reich. It is a photograph of his father's corpse taken shortly after he was hanged at Nuremberg for war crimes in October 1946. Niklas has no illusions regarding his father's part in the mass murder of Polish Jews during the Nazi occupation and once referred to him as 'a slime-hole of a Hitler fanatic'.

Frank thought nothing of taking his five-year-old son Niklas on a tour of one of the camps, where he let him witness the humiliation of the prisoners. Afterwards he shared a cup of cocoa with the boy. Although Niklas remembers witnessing the taunting of concentration camp inmates and his father's cruel laughter, the images that still give him nightmares are those of emaciated bodies piled high in the camp grounds, which he later saw in the post-war German newspapers.

'Some of them were children my own age,' he remembers. 'Underneath was the word Poland. I felt sick. I always thought Poland was ours. The private property of the Frank family.'

Niklas carries a photo of his dead father not only to show his young audience what becomes of those who slavishly and blindly follow a fanatic, but also as a reminder that the man who haunts his dreams is truly dead and cannot harm him now.

'I despise him. He loved Hitler more than he loved his own family.'

Niklas is convinced that his father's devotion to Hitler was more than mere misguided loyalty. He suspects that Frank was a passive homosexual and was enamoured of Hitler.

'I have letters he received from two teachers in Munich that were more than friendly . . . I would have loved it if he could have lived out his desires. Then he wouldn't have made a career as a mass murderer.'

Hitler's Jewish Generals

Germans of mixed racial ancestry were categorized as *Mischlinge* (mixed race) and considered no better than Jews or those of non-white extraction. So it seems inconceivable that more than 150,000 men of Jewish origin, including hundreds whom the Nazis termed 'full Jews', were to be found in Hitler's armed forces.

In the Wehrmacht alone there were two field marshals, 23 colonels and 15 generals of Jewish descent, including Wilhelm Keitel and Erich Raeder. A few even evaded the stringent racial requirements demanded by Himmler and joined the SS, which required applicants to prove their Aryan ancestry as far back as 1750. The majority of these men would have been unaware of their ancestry, until bureaucrats from the Office of Racial Purity informed them that their Aryan origins were being investigated.

Incredibly, Hitler knew that many of his officers had 'questionable' origins and chose to overlook them, approving their promotions and commissions and even countersigning the recommendations for decorations which saw 20 officers of Jewish origin awarded the Knight's Cross, the highest decoration for bravery that the Third Reich could bestow on its soldiers.

In the case of one field marshal, Erhard Milch, whose father was Jewish, Goering knowingly falsified his file by giving the name of Milch's maternal uncle as his real father, having first obtained an affidavit from Clara Milch to that effect. It was only one of many times that Goering was to utter his notorious dictum: 'I will decide who is Jewish and who is not!' However, his background did not save Milch from being sentenced to ten years in prison for war crimes at Nuremberg.

German army personnel records documented 77 cases of high-ranking officers who had received a waiver from Hitler declaring them to be of 'German blood', despite being of Jewish extraction, or married to a Jew. A former Cambridge history student, Bryan Rigg, author of *Hitler's Jewish Soldiers*, claims to be able to add another 60 names from the army, navy and Luftwaffe to that list, having trawled through German army personnel files and interviewed surviving members of the officers' families. Among the interviewees was former West German chancellor Helmut Schmidt, who had been a lieutenant in the Luftwaffe although his grandfather was Jewish, a fact he only learned when he was being considered for promotion in the Hitler Youth.

Among the men Rigg tracked down was a Wehrmacht veteran who travelled to Sachsenhausen concentration camp in 1942, where his Jewish father was being held. It was only on seeing his Iron Cross that an SS officer allowed him to visit the old man, with the warning: 'If you did not have that medal, I would send you where your father is.'

The infamous Nuremberg Laws of 1935 decreed that anyone with at least three Jewish grandparents was a Jew in the eyes of the state and therefore forbidden from serving in the armed forces. In addition, there were two categories of

Mischlinge – those with one and those with two Jewish grandparents. Both categories would be stripped of German citizenship, denied all rights under German law and deemed to be 'subjects of the state'.

In 1940 those men serving in the armed forces who had two Jewish grandparents were dismissed, while those with only one were allowed to remain on condition that they were enlisted men and not officers. The expulsion order was issued three more times during the war as the armed forces weeded out those with various degrees of Jewish blood, but each time Hitler had many reinstated as they were useful to him. However, by 1944 even those whose presence had been 'tolerated' were being dismissed or reassigned to non-strategic posts.

Some of the men did not consider themselves to be of Jewish origin because their ancestry was so remote. Others would have been in denial, having been conditioned to view Jews as *Untermenschen* (subhumans), while a few were practising Jews and lived in constant fear of being denounced.

A number hoped that by serving in the forces they would earn the respect of their comrades and their country. Ilse Korner, widow of Lieutenant Hans Joachim Korner, remembered that her husband 'wanted to distinguish himself through his bravery and willingness to fight as a soldier and, thus, escape the persecution of the Nazis'.

Not all were proud of their heritage. Heinz Löwen denounced his own mother to the Gestapo, falsely claiming that she had been a prostitute so that his father's origins could not be proven and at worst he would be a half-Jew.

Having obtained the necessary certificate of *deutschblütig* (of German blood), he then joined the Waffen SS and was killed on the Russian front.

Arguably the most incredible story concerns a German-Jewish veteran of the First World War, Lieutenant Colonel Dr Ernst Bloch, who had been recruited by Admiral Canaris in 1935 and assigned to the Abwehr (German Military Intelligence).

Bloch was duly given the life-saving *Genehmigung* document signed by Hitler, declaring him to be of 'German blood', but with the usual caveat: 'I, Adolf Hitler, leader of the German nation, approve Major Ernst Bloch to be of German blood. However, after the war, Ernst Bloch will be re-evaluated to see if he is still worthy of such a title.'

In 1939, after the invasion of Poland, Bloch was entrusted with a top secret mission that led to one of the most bizarre episodes of the war. The Abwehr was instructed to rescue an ultra-Orthodox Rabbi, Rebbe Menachem Mendel Schneerson, from Warsaw after the US Secretary of State had petitioned the US Consul General in Berlin to save him by any means possible. The extraordinary request was relayed to Canaris, who agreed to send Major Bloch to Warsaw to locate the Rabbi and bring him out through Latvia, where he would be put on a ship to America. Bloch and his small detachment of soldiers encountered many difficulties, not the least of which was locating the Rabbi who was extremely wary, to say the least, of entrusting his life to German soldiers. But after convincing the Rabbi that they were his only hope of a safe passage through German lines, they were successful in seeing him safely out of the country and aboard a ship bound for the United States.

Bloch was subsequently promoted to lieutenant colonel and awarded the Iron Cross, but in September 1944 Himmler heard of his Jewish parentage and demanded his dismissal.

Hitler's Poster Boy

The Nazis produced some of the most memorable propaganda posters of the period, but a poster they would have liked to forget was one depicting the ideal German soldier. It turned out that the soldier whose photograph had been used, Private Werner Goldberg, was part Jewish. Werner's father had converted to Christianity in order to marry a Gentile, but this did not save him from being dismissed from his government post under the odious Nazi race laws prohibiting Jews from being employed in the civil service.

Werner was therefore acutely aware of his Jewish ancestry but he still enlisted in the Wehrmacht a year before the war and was with his regiment when it invaded Poland in September 1939.

Shortly afterwards his photograph appeared in the *Berliner Tageblatt* under the headline 'The Ideal German Soldier' and was subsequently used on recruitment posters. He might have risen through the ranks had it not been for Hitler's directive of April 1940, which called for all first-degree *Mischlinge* (those with two Jewish grandparents) to be discharged from the army. Werner returned to his job in a clothing factory, but was able to save his father from deportation twice, once by smuggling the old man out of a secure hospital under the noses of the guards and the second time by persuading him to simply ignore a summons from the Gestapo.

Chapter 3

THE GREAT DECEIVER

'[Hitler] was the incarnation of the average . . . the projection of an individual failure on to a whole nation.'

Joachim Fest

On 1 February 1933, Hitler's first day in office, he made the nation the first of many promises that he had no intention of keeping. He affirmed that the regime would 'protect Christianity' and 'safeguard the family', while his underlings were already planning to undermine the authority of the Church by drumming up false corruption charges against the clergy. The Nazis intended replacing Christianity with a neo-pagan cult of National Socialist ideology. They advocated a credo that was the very antithesis of Christian compassion and forgiveness and was founded on the belief that Adolf Hitler was the messiah that Germany had been waiting for and that his iniquitous book *Mein Kampf* should replace the Bible. As for safeguarding the family, the Nazis undermined this institution too. The Labour Front would require men to live separate lives far from home, which put enormous strain on families and resulted in hardship for the wives and mothers who were left to fend for themselves. Nazi indoctrination would also encourage children to inform on their parents and teachers, employees to spy on each other and neighbours to turn against neighbours, as every citizen was obliged to report anti-patriotic statements or comments that might be interpreted as being critical of the regime.

Marriage and family life were further undermined by the Nazis' implementation of the *Lebensborn* programme, which promoted and facilitated loveless sex between members of the SS and suitable partners. These would be young women who had been selected for their racial characteristics and then persuaded that it was their duty to produce future soldiers of the Reich.

A New Spirit of Hope

Frau Krüger had been a believer. Though not an ardent Nazi, she welcomed the announcement of Hitler's succession to power on the night of 30 January 1933 in the belief that it meant the end of the political instability and economic uncertainty that had hung like a dark cloud over the country for the past four years.

That night she listened to the radio with her husband and two teenage children in the front room of their modest terraced house in the Berlin suburb of Eichkamp as the announcer described the scenes outside the Chancellery. His voice breaking with emotion, he conjured up images of the torchlight procession and the surging crowds who were waiting for the Führer to appear on the balcony and address them. He spoke too of the awakening of a new spirit in Germany, a spirit of hope and shared purpose.

The following days saw neighbours and strangers alike greet each other cordially and agree that everything would be different and better from now on. The men talked of the restoration

ALMOST EVERY HOUSE HUNG OUT THE SWASTIKA FLAG. 'SUDDENLY ONE WAS A SOMEBODY ... ON A HIGHER LEVEL – A GERMAN'

of national pride, of Germany having its say in international affairs and a return to full employment. Women looked forward to seeing more than empty shelves in the shops and being able to go about the streets safely without the fear of witnessing violent brawls between the Brownshirts and the Bolsheviks.

Almost every house in Eichkamp hung out the swastika flag. Even children flew a red, white and black Nazi pendant on their bicycles. Frau Krüger bought one for her son Horst from a Jewish street seller, not because she wanted to demonstrate her support for the new administration but simply because she didn't want her son to be the odd one out.

'Suddenly one was a somebody,' Horst later recalled, 'part of a better class of people, on a higher level – a German.'

There were numerous parades to celebrate the new administration and almost daily pronouncements detailing an extensive programme of public works that would put every able-bodied man back in paid employment. The men of the Labour Front marched through the streets with their spades over their shoulders, a conspicuous display of the optimism that galvanized the nation. The country would be linked by a network of major new access roads – the autobahns – making the distribution of goods faster and more cost-efficient. German culture would be exhibited in a suitable setting with the building of new museums, art galleries, theatres and concert halls. Slums and tenements would be torn down and replaced by community housing, and substantial new sports facilities would be constructed to encourage fitness and competitiveness. The quality of life would improve for every citizen of the new Germany. There would be exceptions of course, for the criminals, the malingerers, political opponents and the 'undesirables'.

The good people of Eichkamp knew who the undesirables

were, but it wasn't for them to question the will of the Führer. He knew what was best for the nation and would do what was right. He would rein in the more extreme elements in the Party and tone down the anti-Semitic rhetoric once his cronies took their seats in the Reichstag. President von Hindenburg would not have offered him the chancellorship had he not first had assurances from Herr Hitler that the SA would be subdued and come to heel.

But the SA remained a defiant and uncontrollable element within the Party and being a substantial paramilitary force they posed a serious threat to Hitler's plans to bring the armed forces under his command. It was only after the murder of Röhm and dozens of the SA leadership in June 1934 that the true nature of Hitler's murderous regime was revealed, but by then it was too powerful to be brought down from within.

Even after the Röhm purge, ordinary citizens such as Frau Krüger continued to have faith in the Führer and find excuses for his failure to fulfil his promises.

'We must be patient,' she would say, 'even the Führer cannot work miracles overnight.'

A devout Catholic, she viewed Hitler as the propaganda machine portrayed him; as the devoted son who had nursed his ailing mother in her final days, as the impoverished artist who had overcome his humble origins to devote his life and considerable energies to the well-being of his people and even as the Austrian artist Hubert Lanzinger had depicted him in 1935 – a knight in shining armour leading the sons of Germany to glory against the barbarian hordes to the east. Such a man would not lie to his people.

Hitler did not want war, she told herself, even after her son had been conscripted into the Wehrmacht. Had the Führer not assured them time and again, as he swallowed up his neighbours, that this would be his 'last territorial claim in Europe'?

Reality Check

But after the autobahn network had been constructed, it remained eerily empty, being used only to transport troops and tanks from one end of the country to the other. The slum housing remained long after the ministerial buildings had been occupied and the men of the Labour Front were no longer singing on their way to work, but complaining that they were forced to live away from their families in spartan accommodation. They were poorly paid and were fed food many would have considered no better than prison fare.

The men who built the autobahns received on average two-thirds of the wages they had been earning for comparable work in a factory or on a building site after the compulsory 'contributions' had been deducted, which was significantly less than unemployment benefit.

They worked in all weathers and returned to pass the tedious 'leisure' hours in their unheated barracks, for which they were required to pay 15 pfennigs a day plus another 35 pfennigs for their meagre meals.

Female employees, whether they worked in an office, a shop or a factory, could expect to be paid a third less than their male colleagues, from which five marks would be deducted for their meals. Travel costs would reduce their wage packet significantly if the job entailed working a considerable distance from home.

Women who worked in the private sector were marginally better off than those who were drafted in by the state to work in menial clerical jobs in the various ministries or in manufacturing. If they had been conscripted into employment, female factory workers might find themselves having to report for their 12-hour shift at 6 am, leaving them with no time to do their housework or the shopping. The only women exempt from compulsory service were mothers with young children who were considered to be serving the Fatherland in a way the Führer would approve of. But older women and mothers with children who were old enough to look after themselves were expected to report for compulsory employment and go wherever the administration required them. Many suffered from fatigue, which was exacerbated by lack of sleep when the Allied air raids began.

Women in the Reich

Hitler had made it clear that the National Socialist revolution would be an entirely male event. And yet large numbers of women voted for the Party and turned out to swoon at the Führer's feet. Those who were privileged to present him with a welcoming bouquet of flowers were subsequently treated with excessive reverence by their town or village, as if they had been in the presence of a saint.

But the fact remains that women fared badly under National Socialism in the pre-war years. Unmarried single women were regarded as second-class citizens or *Staatsangehörigen* ('subjects of the state'), and were afforded the same legal status as Jews and the mentally disabled. But they were welcome to work as unpaid activists and many did so, even though they would be given no say in influencing Party policy.

Hitler frowned on women taking an active part in politics or the professions and restricted their access to higher education by imposing a limit on female university applicants. Universities were to accept only one female student for every ten males and frequently they allocated even fewer places to women.

The Nazis envisaged a role for 'the weaker sex' that was confined to the home and the hearth, as expressed in the Party maxim *Kinder, Küche und Kirche* ('Children, Kitchen and Church'). They were encouraged to marry and to produce children for which they would be awarded medals like prize cattle and if they or their husbands were not able to have children of their own they were urged to adopt them.

The state even supplied 'orphans' taken by force from other countries (400,000 in total, half of them from Poland alone) to be fostered by parents who were loyal Party members and didn't ask too many questions concerning the origin of their adopted infants. Their only obligation was to 'Germanize' the children, who had been selected for their Aryan looks and were deemed young enough to accept indoctrination.

> **THE STATE SUPPLIED 'ORPHANS' TAKEN BY FORCE FROM OTHER COUNTRIES TO BE FOSTERED BY PARENTS WHO WERE LOYAL PARTY MEMBERS**

Many of those who were abducted were transported in cattle wagons in which hundreds died from heat in the summer, hypothermia in the winter or thirst and starvation long before they reached their destination. This would be a 'children's education camp' where they were subjected to an intrusive medical examination to determine their 'racial value'. If they were considered suitably 'Nordic', they were then given their new German name and issued with a false birth certificate before being assigned to a distribution centre which would find them a new home.

In a clumsy effort to explain their Polish accents and lack of German vocabulary, the children from Poland were listed as 'Children of German Descent'. Those who resisted were either transported to concentration camps or forced to work as slave labour under their Nazi masters.

Many of the abductees grew up with no memory of their real parents and no knowledge of their true identity.

Workers' Party?

It is a fallacy that the Nazis were a popular working class movement. The largest number of votes for the National Socialists were cast in the rural areas. In the major towns and cities, the Party's popularity was concentrated among the middle class, small business owners, shopkeepers, office workers, teachers and the civil service.

It was industry and big business that supported the NSDAP and profited from Hitler's rearmament programme. During the pre-war years, the wages of skilled workers remained low, falling from 79.2 pfennigs an hour in 1933 to 78.5 by 1937 and then rising to 79.2 in 1939, which was effectively a decrease as prices had significantly increased in that six-year period. Wages for unskilled workers had risen to only 81 pfennigs an hour by 1943, a decade after Hitler's succession, but prices had soared. In that same period profits increased from 6.6 billion marks in 1933 to 15 billion in 1938 and munitions manufacturers and raw materials producers announced a tripling of their returns. The arms manufacturer Flick sold weaponry and munitions at up to 37 per cent more than the pre-war price and made an estimated 8 million mark profit from renting a factory from the regime at a fraction of its true market price.

Unskilled workers had been led to expect that the Nazi leadership would improve their lot once they took power, but those in the Party such as Gregor Strasser, who had fought for workers' rights against the faction led by Hitler, had been ousted or silenced long before 1933.

The Nazis promoted the idea of a classless society in which workers would share a communal meal with their employers, but such events were only staged for the newsreels. In practice, employees were denied a say in wage negotiations and had had no influence on working conditions since Hitler abolished the trade unions. Workers were instead represented by the German Labour Front (DAF), which had acquired the assets of the dissolved unions, making it the only organization that agreed wages with management on behalf of the employees.

During the Hitler years, working hours increased with the introduction of production targets, while wages declined. Only the factory owners, company directors and investors reaped the rewards of rearmament.

The rights of workers were severely restricted under new laws such as the Law for the Organization of National Labour (1934), which gave employers the right to refuse an employee's request to leave. Without the necessary documents which were required by all employers, employees couldn't begin a new job. Strikes were outlawed and all employees had sums deducted from their wages to pay compulsory membership dues to Nazi 'welfare' organizations, which invariably ended up in the pockets of Party officials.

Workers – and unskilled workers in particular – had become mere servants of the state.

But even servants would be allowed a little leisure time.

Strength Through Joy

In November 1933 the Labour Front initiated a programme of organized activities under the banner 'Strength Through Joy' ('*Kraft durch Freude*'), which offered incentives to productivity such as state-subsidized cruises, cultural events and holidays in the German countryside. Millions took advantage of the diverse range of activities on

> ON CRUISE SHIPS, PASSENGERS WERE SUBJECTED TO PROPAGANDA THROUGH LOUDSPEAKERS THAT COULDN'T BE TURNED DOWN OR OFF

offer, but they were in the main the highly skilled who had worked hard to beat production targets, office staff and management.

Few working class families could afford to venture beyond their village, town or city, but with the average wage for a semi-skilled factory worker set at 30 marks a week, even they could afford the cost of a short holiday in the Harz mountains or a week at a resort on the North Sea coast. Needless to say, the regime lost no opportunity to capitalize on the fact that they had a captive audience at these resorts and on board their chartered cruise ships, and subjected them to sustained propaganda through loudspeakers that couldn't be turned down or off.

There were no fewer than 156 loudspeakers on the cruise ship *Robert Ley*, which could carry up to 1,600 passengers to Scandinavia, North Africa, Bulgaria, Italy or Turkey for an average cost of just 200 marks. CBS correspondent William L. Shirer reported on one cruise for his American listeners:

'Though life abroad was organized by Nazi leaders to a point of excruciation, the German workers seemed to have a good time. And at bargain rates! A cruise to Madeira, for instance, cost only $25, including rail fare to and from the German port, and other jaunts were equally inexpensive . . . In winter special skiing excursions to the Bavarian Alps were organized at a cost of $11 a week, including car fare, room and board, rental of skis and lessons from a ski instructor.'

In 1934–35 more than 3 million Germans took part in discounted sports and leisure activities using facilities built by the Social Democrats and the trade unions, who had been organizing such events for free since the late 19th century. However, once Strength Through Joy proved popular, the regime began to build its own 'community villages', where they were able to keep an even closer eye on their residents. Here's a description from Shirer:

'The resort spanned eight kilometres of the Baltic shore, with six-storey residence blocks interspersed with refectories and centred on a huge communal hall designed to accommodate all 20,000 of the resort's holidaymakers as they engaged in a collective demonstration of enthusiasm for the regime and its policies. It was consciously designed for families, to make good the lack of facilities for them in other Strength Through Joy enterprises, and it was intended to be cheap enough for the ordinary worker to afford, at a price of no more than 20 Reichsmarks for a week's stay.'

Labour Front leader Robert Ley explained that 'workers were to gain strength for their work by experiencing joy in their leisure' and though it smacked of regimented leisure time of the kind approved by correctional facilities, there were those in the Nazi leadership who hoped such initiatives would improve the quality of life for employees.

Albert Speer wrote of an initiative launched under the slogan 'Beauty of Labour':

'First we persuaded factory owners to modernize their offices and to have some flowers about. But we did not stop there. Lawn was to take the place of asphalt. What had been wasteland was to be turned into little parks where the workers could sit during breaks. We urged that window areas within factories be enlarged and workers' canteens set up . . . We provided educational movies and a counselling service to help businessmen on questions of illumination and ventilation . . . One and all devoted themselves to the cause of making some improvements in the workers' living conditions and moving closer to the ideal of a classless People's Community.'

Factory workers were placated by relentless promises of new leisure facilities and canteens, only to learn that they were not only expected to build these facilities but they had to pay for them too!

But the most dishonest offer was the promise of the

so-called 'people's car', the Volkswagen, for which a sum was deducted each month from the workers' already dwindling pay packets. Three hundred thousand employees dutifully paid between five and fifteen marks every month over the course of several years, for which they received a numbered voucher and Ley's personal 'guarantee' of a brand new 'Beetle' car.

A private report commissioned by the Social Democrat Party in April 1939 noted:

'For a long time the car was a main topic of conversation in all sections of the population in Germany. All other pressing problems, whether of domestic or foreign policy, were pushed into the background for a while. The grey German everyday sank beneath notice under the impression of this music of the future. Wherever the test models of the new Strength Through Joy construction are seen in Germany, crowds gather around them. The politician who promises a car for everyone is the man of the masses if the masses believe his promises. And as far as the Strength Through Joy car is concerned, the German people do believe in Hitler's promises.'

The accumulated deposits amounted to a considerable income for the fund administrators, who in the event paid nothing out as the car was never produced in quantity. A prototype was exhibited at the Munich and Vienna motor shows in 1938 and Hitler was presented with one the following year, which he gave to Eva Braun. But for the 300,000 workers who had paid their instalments in the belief that they would one day own their own motor car it was just another of

Hitler's broken promises. Long before the first mass-produced vehicle was scheduled to roll off the production line, the Volkswagen factory at Fallersleben had been converted to the manufacture of munitions.

Closed Shop

Shopkeepers and the owners of small businesses were also betrayed by the Party that so many of them had supported and voted for.

The Nazis had promised to end 'unfair competition' by 'Aryanizing' Jewish-owned department stores and businesses, which meant terrorizing the proprietors into abandoning their establishments and fleeing the country or selling them for a token sum to the regime.

But instead of then turning these stores and firms over to their envious German neighbours as they had promised to do, the Nazis installed their cronies and those businessmen who had greased the palms of Party officials in the hope of jumping the queue.

Consequently, the new owners felt under no obligation whatsoever to play fair and often ruthlessly undercut the competition.

Under new Nazi-approved management, the department stores refused to honour the promise made by the previous owners to rent out units to small stallholders and instead squeezed local stores and firms out of business. As the economy deteriorated under the regime, wages fell, prices rose and sales declined, forcing an increasing number of customers to demand goods on credit even though it was unlikely that they would ever be able to repay the debt.

Law and Order

If the average voter had hoped that by putting their cross in the box for the NSDAP candidate they were voting for a 'strong man' who would ensure a return to 'law and order', they were soon disillusioned. Despite the conspicuous presence of the secret police on every street corner and the threat of draconian punishments for the criminal, incidents of rape and murder rose alarmingly during the Hitler years.

> **RATIONING WAS INTRODUCED IN 1939 AND ALMOST IMMEDIATELY IT GAVE RISE TO RACKETEERING AND A THRIVING BLACK MARKET IN COUPONS**

Rationing was introduced in August 1939 and almost immediately it gave rise to racketeering and a thriving black market in coupons, as essentials such as clothes, coffee, basic foodstuffs, shoes and even soap, as well as luxuries, were in short supply and available only with sufficient colour-coded coupons. But the value of these coupons was undermined after the Allies dropped hundreds of thousands of forged coupons in the belief that it would demoralize the population almost as effectively as bombing.

Having enough coupons did not, of course, guarantee that the item would be available and that led to the black market economy where almost everything was obtainable – for a price. But at least there was no queuing, for part of a German housewife's daily routine was to spend hours queuing for goods that were often sold out by the time she reached the counter.

As always in times of shortage, crime increased. Audacious gangs broke into government warehouses and stole rationed provisions, while the price of goods on the black market doubled every year from 1939 to 1944.

Drug dealers, draft dodgers and other opportunists went underground to create an entire subculture based on illicit goods funded by a phantom economy whose principal currency was cigarettes. Fresh eggs, for example, would typically cost four cigarettes. Ironically, an administration that sought to control the ordinary citizen found itself powerless to prevent a once law-abiding population from circumventing the law.

In the last full year of the war the illicit traders were doing business openly on the streets of Berlin and other major cities. It has been estimated that at its peak up to a third of all goods and services in the capital were being traded on the black market.

The administration condemned them as war economy criminals (*Volksschädlinge* or 'folk parasites') although they were more commonly known as *Schieber* ('pushers'). But when it came to a mother providing for her family, or a man acquiring stockings for his mistress, no matter how fervently they supported the regime they would willingly do business with whoever could supply their needs.

It is revealing that those shopping for illicit goods invariably trusted strangers more than their neighbours, who might well inform on them. Eighty per cent of Gestapo investigations were attributed to informers, some of whom might have whispered to the authorities in order to divert suspicion from themselves by demonstrating their loyalty to the regime. More worrying for the regime was the fact that many Nazi Party officials were willing to accept a bribe in cash or illicit goods in return for turning a blind eye to such activities.

Chapter Four

THICK AS THIEVES

Overcoming Opposition

From the earliest days the Nazi leaders were impatient for power. They distrusted and despised the democratic process, and so had no qualms about abusing the voting system.

In the two national elections held in 1932 prior to Hitler's succession to the chancellorship, the Nazis lost 2 million votes, falling from 13.7 million in July 1932 to 11.7 million in November. Even worse, the two workers' parties – the SPD (Social Democratic Party) and the KPD (Communist Party of Germany) – netted 6 per cent more votes in total than the National Socialists in the autumn election. This alarmed the industrialists and the ruling elite, who persuaded President von Hindenburg to appoint Hitler as chancellor. Hindenburg was at first reluctant to appoint a man whose politics he despised, but he relented when he was assured that 'the upstart Austrian corporal' would be kept under the watchful eye of von Papen, a centre party politician and former chancellor, who would serve as vice-chancellor.

But even a year after Hitler had been sworn in, a significant minority still refused to endorse his policies and his party. Although there were to be no more free elections, opposition to the Nazis continued.

In 1933 there were more than 460 street battles between rival factions, in which 400 participants were seriously injured and 80 were killed. When the elderly von Hindenburg died on 2 August 1934, Hitler lost no time in abolishing the office of the presidency and demanding that the Wehrmacht swear a personal oath of allegiance to their new Führer, who was now Supreme Commander of the Armed Forces as well as being Head of State and leader of the only party in the Reichstag.

And still Hitler felt the need to legitimize his stranglehold on power, if only to give the impression to the outside world that he ruled with the will of the people. But the referendum held on 19 August revealed that more than a sixth of those who voted had denied Hitler the endorsement he sought. Despite the propaganda barrage and the intimidating presence of the SA at the polling stations, tens of thousands had voted 'Nein'. In some working class districts the 'no' vote was as much as a third of all votes cast. Admittedly, a proportion of these were protest votes, aimed at drawing Hitler's attention to the anger many working class Party members felt at his failure to deal with the corruption endemic within his party.

MEMBERS ASKED WHY HITLER HAD FAILED TO ACT TO PREVENT THE ABUSE OF POWER AND PRIVILEGE AMONG PARTY OFFICIALS

Eighteen months later, in March 1936, a Gestapo report revealed that there was still dissatisfaction among ordinary Party members, who asked why Hitler had failed to act to prevent the abuse of power and privilege among Party officials. Many loyal members were becoming impatient with the leadership, who appeared to be indifferent to their difficulties as prices continued to rise, while wages remained comparatively low and scarcities made providing for their families more difficult every day.

But shortly after the report was compiled, on 7 March,

German troops marched unopposed into the Rhineland to reclaim territory occupied by the French under the terms of the hated Versailles Treaty. It was unknown at the time that the Wehrmacht had orders to retreat if the French showed the least sign of resisting, but they simply stood by and watched the German troops march past. The audacious coup bolstered Hitler's popularity within Germany and pacified many of those at home and abroad who had voiced concerns over his aggressive rhetoric.

Ballot Rigging

Although the regime could claim to have won the hearts and minds of the masses they still feared those who stubbornly refused to submit to intimidation. The obvious solution as they saw it was to rig the results in their favour, but the men they entrusted with the task were not the brightest minds they could find. The March 1936 election exposed their fraudulent tactics when the official result was declared for Berlin, because 99 per cent of the votes in every district of the capital went to the Nazis.

In Friedrichshagen, 15 voting centres recorded a suspiciously high 100 per cent turnout and the remaining five centres had only one vote less than the total population of the district. As Gauleiter of Berlin, Dr Goebbels made his displeasure known to Party activists. Did they want the foreign press to compare German elections with the notorious rigged ballot organized by gangster Al Capone in Cicero in 1924, when he installed a puppet administration to legalize his gambling activities in the Chicago suburb?

In Hamburg that same month ballot papers for the national

plebiscite on Germany's reoccupation of the Rhineland had been numbered in invisible ink so that Brownshirt thugs could identify those who had voted '*Nein*'.

It took courage to be seen to be taking too close an interest in the results, but trainee lawyer Peter Bielenberg volunteered to assist with the count in his district of Berlin at a later referendum that year and was heartened to discover that hundreds of his fellow citizens had voted against the new administration. However, the next morning the newspapers declared a unanimous vote in favour of the Party's policies, confirming what Peter and other liberal-minded Germans had feared: that opposition had been effectively silenced and there would be no hope of ousting the dictator by democratic means.

Although subsequent improvements in the economy and a decline in unemployment were due to external factors and the achievements of the much-vaunted public works programme had been instigated by the previous administration, Hitler took sole credit for them. In a speech to the Reichstag in April 1939, he boasted of restoring German pride and reclaiming its 'stolen' territory. In doing so, he identified his will with that of Germany:

'I overcame chaos in Germany, restored order, enormously raised production in all fields of our national economy . . . I succeeded in completely resettling in useful production those 7 million unemployed who so touched our hearts . . . I have not only politically united the German nation but also rearmed it militarily, and I have further tried to liquidate that Treaty sheet by sheet whose 448 Articles contain the vilest rape that nations and human beings have ever been expected to submit to. I have restored to the Reich the provinces grabbed from us in 1919; I have led millions of deeply unhappy Germans, who have been snatched away from us, back into the Fatherland; I have restored the thousand-year-old historical unity of German living space; and I have attempted to accomplish all that without shedding blood and without inflicting the sufferings of war on my people or any other.'

Once in power, the Nazis determined that they would remain so and doctored the wording of each plebiscite or referendum to ensure they obtained the result they required – a unanimous '*Ja!*' for whatever the Führer proposed.

The *Anschluss* with Austria in March 1938 can be seen as a typical instance.

The question asked of every German citizen with the right to vote (Jews excluded) was: 'Do you approve of the reunification of Austria with the German Reich that was enacted on 13 March 1938 and do you vote for the party of our leader, Adolf Hitler? Yes. No.'

It combined two separate issues – a statement of support, or not, for the recent annexation of Austria, which no 'loyal' citizen of the Reich would dare to deny was a triumph for Hitler, and a vote for or against the Nazi Party – but only one answer could be given. The design of the ballot paper also 'encouraged' the voter to tick the '*Ja*' box, which was printed within a larger circle than the '*Nein*', while Hitler's name was in larger type, emphasizing his importance. The official result was a 99 per cent vote in favour of Hitler's actions.

The Great Bullion Robbery

When Hitler drove through the streets of Vienna in an open-top Mercedes on 15 March 1938 to celebrate the *Anschluss* (Austria's union with Germany), he was greeted by scenes of mass adulation that even he could never have envisaged.

It had been a lifelong dream of the former corporal from Braunau am Inn to be hailed as the conquering hero who would bring Austria 'home' to the Reich. He had finally been able to restore the pride of his homeland, which had been humiliated by the punitive conditions imposed by the Versailles Treaty (including a bill for 132 billion marks which was later renegotiated down to 112 billion). But if the adoring crowds on the Heldenplatz had known what had been done under the cover of the *Anschluss*, they might not have been so eager to welcome him.

In the preceding hours, Hitler's associates had stripped the Austrian Central Bank of its assets, namely 100 tons of gold bullion, and shipped it back to Berlin. An additional 5.7 tons was transferred from London, where it had been held for safekeeping. Within a matter of hours the Nazis had increased Germany's reserves fourfold. Then on 23 March 1938 the regime decreed that all Jewish inhabitants of the Reich were to declare the value of their property and private assets including stocks, bonds and personal valuables. This law had been enacted in anticipation of confiscating an estimated 4 billion Reichsmarks from Austria's Jewish population following the annexation. The regime set up a clearing bank to launder their ill-gotten gains, which they cynically named The National Bank of Austria in Liquidation, to give the impression that the deposits were merely a part of the assimilation process. By these means 14.3 tons of gold were acquired from Austria's Jews. This included 65 million Reichsmarks in gold coins, 299 million in stocks and bonds, 150 million in foreign shares and 345 million in gold and currency held by the Austrian National Bank.

The following February all Jews in the Reich were ordered to hand in their jewellery, silverware and gold to the municipal pawnshops, for which they would receive a token fee. In this way the regime acquired the wealth of some of its most affluent citizens for a fraction of its true value. All the gold was subsequently smelted into anonymous and untraceable gold bars, which were deposited in the Reichsbank.

Cash Not Accepted

Without gold reserves, the Nazis knew they could not sustain the war that Hitler was planning. The gold would buy the raw materials that Germany needed to manufacture tanks, planes and ships and also the oil to fuel them. Germany had begun to make low-grade synthetic oil, but it was high-grade oil that would lubricate the wheels of the military machine. And that was produced by its Axis ally, Romania.

Franco's fascist regime would supply the tungsten that would be needed to process low-grade German iron ore into steel, but Spain would need to be paid, despite the debt that Franco owed Hitler for turning the tide of the Spanish Civil War. Turkey would supply the Nazi state with chromium (essential in the manufacture of tanks, shells and U-boats) and Sweden would send iron ore and ball bearings, but neither country would accept cash because exchange rates could fluctuate wildly once war was declared. The significance of these raw materials to Germany's plans for conquest is often underestimated, but according to a memo written by Albert Speer to Hitler on 10 November 1943, if the supply of chromium from Turkey had been blocked Germany would have exhausted its stockpile within six months and the manufacture of armaments would have come to a grinding halt within four to twelve weeks.

Politically neutral Portugal was the second-largest trading partner that Germany could still count on at the time, but they too insisted on being paid in gold once they discovered that the Nazis had been paying them in counterfeit cash. Gold was the international currency and Germany intended to hoard as much of it as it could.

Going for Gold

Hjalmar Schacht, Hitler's finance minister and president of the Reichsbank, knew exactly how much bullion was being held in Austria's Central Bank and in Britain because he also happened to be a founding director of the Bank of International Settlements (BIS), whose members were obliged to declare details of their assets to fellow members.

Schacht's role in assisting the regime should not be underestimated. American ambassador William Dodd referred to Schacht as 'the economic dictator' of Germany, while the American consul general in Berlin later declared:

'If it had not been for his efforts[. . .]the Nazi regime would have been unable to maintain itself in power and establish its control over Germany, much less to create the enormous war machine which was necessary for its objectives in Europe and later throughout the world.'

An unprincipled opportunist, Schacht had been hired by Hitler for his 'consummate skill at swindling other people' and for that reason he did not press him to join the Party. Schacht was instrumental in raising the enormous sums that financed the Nazis' election campaigns between 1926 and 1932

AN UNPRINCIPLED OPPORTUNIST, SCHACHT HAD BEEN HIRED BY HITLER FOR HIS 'CONSUMMATE SKILL AT SWINDLING OTHER PEOPLE'

and he played a significant role in manoeuvring Hitler into a position where he could be offered the chancellorship. He had urged Franz von Papen to resign in favour of Hitler, of whom he said: 'Hitler is the only man who can save Germany.' But in reality Schacht thought Hitler was 'half-educated' and he had only contempt for the SA, whom he dismissed as brutes.

In 1931 Schacht told an American journalist that if the Nazis came to power they would be incapable of running the economy. 'The Nazis cannot rule,' he told her, 'but I can rule through them.'

Schacht persuaded Hitler not to make any economic pledges or commit the Party to a particular programme in the months leading up to his succession to the chancellorship as he would not be able to defend his position or explain why he considered it prudent.

He was one of the few men in the administration to voice opposition to Hitler's plans for war, but only on the grounds that it would prove disastrous for the economy. When he saw that Hitler could not be dissuaded, Schacht devised a plan to safeguard Germany's finances during the conflict. Central to this strategy was the founding in 1930 of the BIS, which was based in neutral Switzerland under the pretence that it would facilitate the payment of Germany's reparations bill. Schacht was to be its first president and the man who ensured that the gold reserves of conquered countries would be deposited in the Reichsbank, because his position enabled him to use the BIS as a clearing house for both Germany and its victims.

This proved crucial in the case of Czechoslovakia, which had entrusted its total reserves – £6m/$8m in gold – to the Bank of England. The British could have withheld the money under the circumstances, but as soon as Prague capitulated Schacht requested that the Czech bullion be deposited in the Reichsbank and, incredibly, the British complied. By seizing the defeated nation's gold reserves, the Third Reich destabilized its economy and destroyed confidence in its currency, whose value plummeted.

Gold also financed the pro-Nazi parties in the neighbouring countries that Germany intended to invade. But first they needed to undermine resistance in those countries by spreading Nazi ideology among their extreme nationalists and buying the loyalty of collaborators.

Schacht's money-raising schemes did not stop there, for it was he, a rabid anti-Semite, who conceived the odious notion of forcing Jews to pay an emigration tax to leave Germany for safer shores and who organized the funnelling of enormous funds from overseas to pay for Hitler's public works programme.

The building of the autobahn network, which was much admired by Germany's foreign friends, and the massive rearmament programme, which alarmed its neighbours, were both financed by overseas loans which Hitler had no intention of repaying. He had pushed through the building of the autobahns at a cost of 600 million Reichsmarks because he needed to be able to move troops and tanks quickly from one part of the country to the other and not because he wanted to assist German industry or facilitate travel for the general population.

While the German armed forces flaunted their superiority in orchestrated displays of military pageantry for the newsreel cameras at the annual Party rallies at Nuremberg, the regime was practically bankrupt. It was primarily the theft of the Austrian gold reserves that kept the creditors at bay until Hitler could launch his war and empty the bank vaults of the defeated nations.

Reichsbank vice-president Emil Puhl wrote a revealing memo that autumn:

'The rapid implementation of rearmament was only possible because of the use of available gold, foreign exchange from the former Reich, and the immediate recovery of Austrian gold, foreign raw material, and valuable securities reserves.'

The Four-Year Plan

According to writer George M. Taber, author of *Chasing Gold*, German rearmament was funded primarily through the issuing of promissory notes in excess of the 100 million mark limit imposed on the Central Bank by German law. These notes were issued through a dummy corporation set up by Schacht under the name *Metallurgische Forschungsgesellschaft* (Metal Research Company).

Mefo, as it was popularly known, had no employees but capital of 100 million marks donated by four major German firms. The armaments manufacturers would be paid in Mefo currency which would accrue 4 per cent interest per annum over four years, after which they would be repaid in full by the Reichsbank. However, the Nazis had no intention of honouring this 'investment' and soon extended the repayment period to 17 years. Schacht thought the scheme 'ingenious' and took delight in knowing that foreign investors had been fooled into buying Mefo bills without being aware of where their money was going.

In May 1935 Schacht reported to Hitler: 'Our armaments are, therefore, being financed partially with the assets of our political opponents.'

Over the following five years, Germany spent 20.5 billion Reichsmarks on rearmament of which 12 billion had been obtained through the sale of Mefo bills. But within a year Hitler no longer felt indebted to Schacht and was becoming irritated by some of the banker's outspoken opinions on National Socialist policy, which he made in the pages of the foreign press and in speeches at official government functions. In August 1936 Schacht was effectively sidelined by Goering, whom Hitler had entrusted with implementing the so-called Four Year Plan. This 13-page memo, which Hitler had drafted that summer, was primarily directed towards facilitating the rearmament of Germany and making the economy self-sufficient in preparation for the war he envisaged launching no later than 1940.

In order to be economically self-sufficient, Germany had to be capable of producing all the raw materials and fuel it required. What it couldn't manufacture or import in sufficient quantities it would have to be able to produce synthetically, specifically rubber from the plentiful brown coal that I. G. Farben had been insisting it could process. Foreign currency would be accumulated so that Germany could pay for imports if the emergency arose, but the question of production costs incurred in the manufacture of three essential raw materials (rubber, iron ore and petroleum) was 'of no consequence', as the regime would not be obliged to pay for them. Besides, Germany would then have at its disposal the natural resources and assets of the occupied countries with which to settle its debts, should it wish to do so, gold being the most significant.

Hitler knew that Schacht would have protested that these targets were impractical and that is why he did not consult him, but instead marginalized him as he did with all functionaries who had outlived their usefulness. When Schacht learned of the Four-Year Plan at a meeting of the cabinet's executive committee chaired by Goering, he telephoned the War Ministry and pleaded with General Blomberg's economic adviser, General Thomas, to persuade Blomberg to intervene. But Blomberg brushed aside Schacht's concerns and told him to have faith in the Führer.

For Goering, the Four-Year Plan brought an unexpected windfall. The iron ore and steel company in Salzgitter which bore his name was now the beneficiary of considerable government funds. By the end of 1941 it was the largest corporation in Europe, having acquired facilities in the conquered countries and moved into the manufacture of armaments. However, according to writer George M. Taber, it proved too unwieldy to manage efficiently and the coal, iron and steel divisions lost money during the war.

Goering was unperturbed. He had had the foresight to open an account in the Reichsbank, where the stolen gold from the conquered countries would be deposited, and he would transfer as much as he wished to his personal account without questions being asked.

To this hoard was added the contents of rifled safety deposit boxes and valuables taken from the homes of wealthy individuals who had been identified as worthy of a visit by the DSK (*Devisenschutzkommando*), Goering's official plain-clothed thieves. In the wake of the Wehrmacht's victories in May 1940, the DSK passed through northern Europe like a plague of locusts, accumulating almost £850 million ($1,000m) in looted valuables and currency, of which £17 million ($22m) was netted in northern France, £117 million ($150m) in the Netherlands and £713 million ($910m) in Belgium.

After the fall of Czechoslovakia several countries thought it prudent to ship their gold reserves to Canada or America, far from Goering's grasp. The Vatican was one of the few sovereign states to save its gold by shipping its entire reserve – amounting to 8 tons of gold bullion – to the safety of the vaults of the New York Federal Reserve. The Bigelow report in 1946 revealed that the Vatican had also received 350 million Swiss francs in looted Nazi gold, which it refused to hand back to Holocaust survivors after the war.

It is estimated that the Nazis managed to plunder gold worth nearly £500 million ($640m) between 1938 and 1945, only half of which they spent before the end of the war. The remaining balance would have been sufficient to prolong the conflict by at least another five years. And had they succeeded in defeating Russia, the Germans would have possessed another 2,800 tons of gold bullion, with which they could have delayed their defeat indefinitely.

THE NAZIS MANAGED TO PLUNDER GOLD WORTH NEARLY £500 MILLION BETWEEN 1938 AND 1945, ONLY HALF OF WHICH THEY SPENT

Profiting from the Final Solution

The crimes of the Third Reich were committed in the name of Adolf Hitler and justified by the perpetrators as having been sanctioned by the Führer. 'I was only following orders' became the default defence of every war criminal who attempted to avoid personal responsibility for their heinous acts. But many aided and abetted robbery, torture, intimidation and murder on their own initiative, exploiting their power and authority to enrich themselves, to exercise control over others and to satisfy their personal grievances.

Hitler's turbulent personality craved conflict and power, and the regime he led became the projection of his own amoral, aberrant personality. In such an environment corruption and criminality proliferated, no more so than in the forced labour, concentration and extermination camps where Hitler's pathological hatred of the Jews and other 'undesirable' elements manifested itself in unspeakable brutality and unconcealed greed.

Double Life of Rudolf Hoess

Rudolf Hoess, commandant of Auschwitz, led two distinctly separate lives. His children remember him as being a strict but loving father who only lost his temper with them once, when they were trying to pull down the fence that divided their villa from the camp where as many as 12,000 victims were gassed and incinerated every day. It was apparently then that he told them that they should never hurt other people.

Hoess would come back to the house at the end of each day to share a meal with his wife and five children, while the prisoners starved to death within sight and sound of the house. Inge-Birgitt was six in 1940, when her father was appointed commandant, and remembers watching smoke rising from the crematorium and wondering what the barbed wire fences and guard towers were for. But her father only discussed family matters when he was off duty. At weekends he worked in the garden like a respectable civil servant.

However, in private he took a pride in 'running the greatest human destruction machine of all time', and confided as much to his diary. He had no qualms about having his family waited on by prisoners or furnishing the villa with furniture and paintings taken from Jews who had died only 100 metres away on the other side of the garden fence.

His wife Hedwig also saw no reason why she should not profit from her husband's position and the opportunities that fate had sent her way. Her wardrobe was stacked with shoes and handbags abandoned by the more affluent women who had ended their journey at Auschwitz.

When the Hoess family fled the advancing Russians in the winter of 1944, they loaded two wagons with stolen goods, but were soon parted from them and forced to hole up at a sugar factory while Hoess worked as a farm labourer under a false name.

When he was finally captured and brought to Nuremberg to testify at the trials of Ernst Kaltenbrunner, Oswald Pohl and the directors of I. G. Farben, he spoke of his efficiency and the operation he had supervised with barely concealed pride. It was he who had successfully persuaded the regime to use I. G. Farben's pesticide Zyklon B for mass extermination purposes, because it 'only' took between three and fifteen minutes for it to achieve its deadly purpose.

'We knew when the people were dead because they stopped screaming . . . Another improvement we made over Treblinka was that we built our gas chambers to accommodate 2,000 people at one time, whereas at Treblinka their ten gas chambers only accommodated 200 people each. The way we selected our victims was as follows: we had two SS doctors on duty at Auschwitz to examine the incoming transports of prisoners. The prisoners would be marched by one of the doctors who would make spot decisions as they walked by. Those who were fit for work were sent into the Camp. Others were sent immediately to the extermination plants. Children of tender years were invariably exterminated, since by reason of their youth they were unable to work. Still another improvement we made over Treblinka was that at Treblinka the victims almost always knew that they were to be exterminated and at Auschwitz we endeavoured to fool the victims into thinking that they were to go through a delousing process. Of course, frequently they realized our true intentions and we sometimes had riots and difficulties due to that fact. Very frequently women would hide their children under their clothes but of course when we found them we would send the children in to be exterminated. We were required to carry out these exterminations in secrecy but of course the foul and nauseating stench from the continuous burning of bodies permeated the entire area and all of the people living in the surrounding communities knew that exterminations were going on at Auschwitz.'

His only regret, he confessed, was having defied his strict Catholic father, who had wanted his son to enter the priesthood.

Everyone Looted

This twisted logic was typical of the irrational mindset that persisted among many of the Nazi leadership and their functionaries, who sought to reconcile their principles with their amoral actions.

Himmler expressed similar sentiments in a speech to SS group leaders in Posen on 4 October 1943, in which he sought to stiffen his men's resolve to participate in the mass murder of men, women and children in the camps which operated under the control of the SS.

'We have the moral right,' he told them, 'we have the duty towards our people, to kill this people which wanted to kill us. But we do not have the right to enrich ourselves with so much as a fur, with a watch, with a mark or with a cigarette or with anything else.'

Those who were found to have robbed the victims would be executed, for they had betrayed their brotherhood and stolen from the Führer to whom they had sworn an oath of loyalty.

The 'Final Solution' was founded on a whole raft of fallacies, not the least of which was Himmler's claim that the Jews would have massacred the Germans if they hadn't been eliminated first. Quite apart from the fact that a significant number of Jews were already assimilated into German society through marriage and would have been hardly discernible as a separate element by the end of the 20th century, they were not a collective group who plotted against their neighbours.

It was therefore necessary for the Nazis to promote the unfounded idea of an imminent Jewish 'threat', which could only be countered by pre-emptive action. But as more than one individual who was a witness to the 'processing' of the camp victims has observed, at the time it looked as if the whole system

THE SS GUARDS HELPED THEMSELVES TO THE MOUNTAIN OF VALUABLES LEFT BEHIND ON THE RAMP (PLATFORM) BY NEW ARRIVALS

had been set in motion in order to separate the Jews of Europe from their property and possessions. Only Hitler appeared to have no desire to profit financially from the elimination of his imaginary enemies.

The SS proved themselves to be the very antithesis of the Teutonic Knights that the former chicken farmer Himmler envisaged them to be. Apart from presiding over many of the worst atrocities of the war (for which they were branded a criminal organization at Nuremberg), the SS condemned themselves by the numerous incidents of theft and corruption recorded by their own courts, which far outnumbered the crimes committed by members of the Wehrmacht.

In the camps the SS guards helped themselves to the mountain of valuables left behind on the ramp (platform) by new arrivals. If they didn't pocket them, they argued, the Ukrainian and Lithuanian guards or the local inhabitants would have done so. Auschwitz administrator Franz Hofbauer boasted of picking up 10,000 Reichsmarks in a single day. Even the train drivers took the opportunity to supplement their pay by lingering around the ramp until the guards had gone, while pretending to tinker with their engine, in the hope of picking up some overlooked jewellery or cash.

The more affluent victims brought jewellery, watches and other valuables with them in the belief that they were being deported to the East where they would begin a new life under the supervision of their German masters. Some brought what little cash they had managed to save sewn into the linings of their coats. The Germans discovered this ruse early on and had a group of prisoners sort through the discarded clothes and rip up any that might contain currency. At a wool combing plant in Bremen, coins were found in the braided hair that had been cut from several young women at Auschwitz.

German currency was deposited in a designated WVHA (Wirtschafts-Verwaltungshauptamt) account. (The WVHA was the Administration and Economic Office of the SS, which served as a 'clearing house' for everything taken from the victims of the camps, as one American judge described it at the post-war trial of WVHA chief Oswald Pohl.) The remainder was divided up among the guards. There was such a large amount of discarded cash that on one occasion an emissary was sent from Berlin to Treblinka to collect a million marks and bring it back in a suitcase to line the pockets of an unnamed Nazi official.

There were mountains of food too, with the choicer items being distributed among the SS, their Ukrainian and Lithuanian collaborators and the commandants, who stocked their larders with meat, cheese, sugar and chocolate that they wouldn't have been able to buy in such quantities and so readily on the thriving black market.

After being herded off the ramp the new intake would be subjected to a selection process and those who were deemed too young, too old or unfit to work were sent through 'the tube', a barbed wire path leading to the 'showers'. There they were ordered to undress and leave their glasses, watches and shoes. Even gold fountain pens were considered of value to the SS, along with broken or damaged watches which were repaired by prisoners in Sachsenhausen before being distributed to officers and men of the armed forces.

The clothes of the victims were collected and fumigated and the yellow stars torn off before being stacked in huts and barracks awaiting shipment to various agencies approved by the Reich Economic Ministry. Some went to the Ethnic German Liaison Office, another SS enterprise which supported the settlement of ethnic Germans in the occupied territories to the east. As Nikolaus Wachsmann observed in *KL: A History of the Concentration Camps*, in this way many German settlers not only took over the homes and farms of evicted Jews but also their clothes.

After each group of new arrivals had been killed a group of prisoners known as the *Sonderkommando* searched the bodies for hidden valuables, removing rings and earrings before tearing gold fillings from their mouths. In the second half of 1944, 90 pounds of gold and white metal was extracted from the victims at Auschwitz alone, according to a secret report compiled by the prisoners. Nothing of value was to be incinerated with the bodies. The women's hair was cut and collected for stuffing mattresses and for making into thread and socks by private firms under the supervision of the Reich Economic Ministry.

The Polish composer Henryk Górecki remembers being taken to Auschwitz by his school when he was 12 years old. He was told that human ashes had been scattered on the ground between the huts as fertilizer, where cabbages were grown, and saw for himself that crushed human bones were 'thrown on the path like shingle'.

All that remained unclaimed were the personal photographs and letters. These too were burned.

Nevertheless, it was thought prudent to murder members of the *Sonderkommando* periodically and replace them with new prisoners to ensure there were no witnesses to what had taken place.

Murder Incorporated

The SS conducted their business in the open. There was no need for secrecy or subterfuge. All proceeds from the death camps were dutifully recorded and deposited in the Reichsbank, which credited the WVHA account with the monetary equivalent of the stolen goods. The account had been opened in the name of SS Hauptsturmführer Bruno Melmer, because it was he who transported the loot from WVHA headquarters in Berlin to the bank, a trip he made 76 times between the summer of 1942 and late 1944.

Other SS accounts used fictional names such as Max Heiliger (Saint Max) and were recorded as *Reinhardfonds* ('funds from Operation Reinhard') or *Besitz der umgesiedelten Juden* ('the property of resettled Jews'). The bank was charged with selling the jewellery and other personal items to pawnshops in Berlin and depositing the proceeds in the SS accounts, so its protestations of ignorance after the war were unpersuasive.

In addition to the crates of valuables taken from the victims, there were hundreds of gold bars that had been smelted by the Prussian Mint. Bank officials saw no reason to question where the gold and other goods originated and pleaded ignorance when they were asked to account for their complicity in the theft after the war. When Walther Funk, president of the Reichsbank, testified at Nuremberg in 1946, he defended the bank's participation in genocide by claiming that many people deposited their valuables in the vault and that the bank was not required to ask how they had come by them.

The prosecutor then asked: 'Were you in the habit of having gold teeth deposited in the Reichsbank?'

Funk could only mutter 'No' and denied knowing the contents of the sealed bags and crates being held in his vaults. He later admitted: 'I am guilty of one thing – that I should have cleared out and not had anything to do with these criminals in the first place.'

In *KL* Wachsmann estimates that the total value of SS 'booty' taken from Auschwitz and Majdanek alone is 'likely to have amounted to several hundred million Reichsmarks', but notes that some of their enterprises made little economic sense. He gives the example of processing the hair from Majdanek prisoners between September 1942 and June 1944, which raised a paltry 365 marks, less than the value of a single gold cigarette case acquired during Operation Reinhard, the code name given to the plan to exterminate Polish Jews in the death camps at Sobibor, Belzec and Treblinka.

Contrary to popular belief, the SS did not profit financially from the lease of inmates to the forced labour programme as much as has been suggested. Although the total income from leasing slave workers to Speer's armaments ministry netted an estimated 200 million marks in 1943 and between 400 and 500 million the following year, this money went to the Chancellery. Himmler was persuaded not to protest too much as the prisoners (whom he described as 'the largest reservoir of manpower') were technically the property of the state and there could be advantages for the SS if they complied with Speer's department. Industry might look favourably upon any requests for new weaponry submitted by the Reichsführer and Himmler would have more political clout if the war economy was dependent on his co-operation.

Corruption in the Camps

As if conditions inside the camps were not horrific enough, some of the SS staff inflicted further privations on the prisoners by stealing their meagre rations and selling these on the black market. Others, such as the sadistic Amon Goeth, commandant of Plaszow, fed meat to his dogs that had been intended for prisoners. He was eventually dismissed from his post by his superiors for hoarding valuables that should have been handed over to the SS. After being declared insane he was committed to an asylum where he remained until he was liberated by the Allies, who tried and executed him for war crimes.

> **SS STAFF STOLE PRISONERS' RATIONS AND SOLD THEM ON THE BLACK MARKET. AMON GOETH FED MEAT INTENDED FOR PRISONERS TO HIS DOGS**

Members of Himmler's elite, the brotherhood of 'decent' men as he called them, claimed they would spare prisoners from a beating or a work detail if they could pay, while others offered to deliver personal messages for a price. Some even deprived prisoners of a change of clothing by selling their unused underwear for a few marks to the locals, but they also sold items earmarked for other prisoners to those inmates who had managed to conceal something worth bartering.

And they knew that they were under no obligation to fulfil their part of the bargain.

The SS may have taken Himmler's speeches seriously and swallowed the indoctrination programme at the SS training schools, but as soon as they were transferred to the camps they saw that their superiors were as likely to be as corrupt as anyone else.

Theodor Eicke, the man whom Himmler entrusted with reorganizing the camps under the command of the SS in May 1934, kept a secret bank account to siphon off funds while urging his men to conform to the highest ideals of the SS. He is reputed to be the man who shot Ernst Röhm in his cell on the Night of the Long Knives and was said to have been second only to Himmler in his fanatical devotion to the SS 'code of honour'.

In March 1933, only a year before Himmler appointed him commander of Dachau and inspector general of the concentration camps, he was confined in a psychiatric clinic after being declared a violent and 'dangerous lunatic'. (The psychiatrist who considered him fit for discharge was Dr Werner Heyde, who became the director of the Nazi euthanasia programme.) Eicke encouraged his men to be brutal and told them not to intervene when prisoners rushed the electrified fences in a desperate attempt to end their ordeal.

He also ordered his guards to witness public floggings to harden them and according to one writer, Thomas Laqueur, fostered 'a homoerotic camp culture rooted in brutality'.

One of Eicke's acolytes was Rudolf Hoess, the future commandant of Auschwitz.

Introduction of the Gas Chambers

At first the camps were inefficient in their chosen methods of extermination. Commandants were made aware that their superiors were becoming impatient, and so in desperation they experimented with various methods.

At Sachsenhausen, Eicke was a witness to the efficiency of the soundproof killing booth, which prisoners of war (POWs) entered in the belief that they were to be given a medical examination. They took their seat on a bench and were then shot in the back of the head through a small aperture in the booth. Three hundred men were murdered in this way in a single day but Eicke was not impressed. On his return to Dachau he resorted to the old-fashioned method – gathering a group of victims in an open field and mowing them down with machine guns. He disposed of 4,000 POWs between September 1941 and June 1942 in this manner. But it was not enough to satisfy his superiors.

The commandants of Flossenbürg and Gross-Rosen preferred lethal injections, the method approved by the organizers of the T4 Euthanasia Programme, but these proved too costly and time-consuming. It was not until the introduction of the purpose-built gas chamber in September 1941 that the Nazis realized they had found the solution they sought. In one trial, hundreds of Soviet POWs were gassed at Auschwitz using Zyklon B crystals, a cyanide-based pesticide. But there were complications. The gas didn't clear fast enough due to poor ventilation and the bodies had to be transported one at a time to the incinerators, or 'the roasts' as the operators called them. The solution was simple. Gas chambers would have to be built with suitable ventilation and crematoria constructed on the same site.

By the end of the year gas chambers had become a feature of many extermination camps. Two problems remained, however. How to condition the guards to participate in the mass murder of civilians hour after hour, day after day, and how to herd the victims into the gas chambers without the risk of resistance.

Dubious Prisoner Incentives

Eicke's contempt for the inmates encouraged his men to abuse and exploit them. The word soon spread among the camps that Inspector General Eicke would look favourably on those who discharged their duties without pity.

After the influx of 'November Jews' at Buchenwald, so called because they were rounded up and imprisoned the morning after *Kristallnacht*, SS men went on a spending spree, buying expensive clothes and luxury cars with the 'donations' they had obtained from the new intake.

However, money was not the only form of currency to be extracted from vulnerable inmates. The introduction of brothels (known as *Sonderbauten*, or 'special buildings') in the camps from October 1941 was another of Himmler's perverse initiatives. He imagined that emaciated and starving men who were living every day in fear of their lives could be persuaded to work even harder by offering them the incentive of sex. In practice few were willing to make use of the facility, which was made all the more unappealing by having to submit to a humiliating procedure requiring a medical examination and the writing of a letter to the commandant to ask permission. Often those who persisted were the privileged Kapos, who ran the gauntlet of angry inmates whenever they visited the designated building on the far edge of the camp.

Other incentives included the 'privilege' of being permitted to write more letters to surviving relatives (with no guarantee that they would still be alive to read them), extra rations, nominal payments, practically worthless vouchers and cigarettes. The latter were only issued to male prisoners as Himmler frowned on the idea of female prisoners being allowed to smoke. Inevitably, once the prisoners obtained any of these dubious incentives, they were subject to abuse by their guards who threatened to withhold them if they didn't do as they ordered or who pocketed them out of spite.

Prisoners were reduced to stealing from each other in order to survive one more day. In Majdanek many were reduced to trading their clothes and shoes for a cup of water from their guards, while a large number died of thirst. For those who were transported to the camps and survived, whether they were Jews, Gypsies, persecuted homosexuals, Jehovah's Witnesses or political prisoners, it was unremitting hell on earth. But for the commandant, his staff and the SS it was, as Franz Stangl, commandant of Treblinka, termed it, 'the happy times'.

Purpose of the Camps

Historian and documentary filmmaker Laurence Rees concluded that Auschwitz and the other camps were conceived primarily as revenue-making industrial centres designed to wring the maximum profit from an endlessly replenishable, unpaid labour force. The fact that the camps also provided an economical means of disposing of the Jews and other 'undesirable elements' was a bonus.

Although Rees does not say so, the guards and the functionaries were conditioned to regard their role as no more than supervisors of an industrial process in which efficiency and productivity were paramount. Their barely concealed enthusiasm for their 'work' and the lack of humanity they displayed in the performance of their duties betrays the degree to which they had been indoctrinated by Nazi ideology. Although many of those employed in the camps were indifferent to what they witnessed, others evidently used their authority as an outlet for their latent sadism and their desire to humiliate, dominate and degrade those they despised, be they Jews, homosexuals, or anyone who dared to look them in the eye.

Goering had originally envisaged the sites as punitive 'boot camps' for political prisoners, opponents and dissenters, but this concept had long been superseded by the compulsion to find a 'Final Solution' to their Führer's pathological obsession with the Jews and the desire of his followers to profit by it, whether financially or by gratifying their own twisted desires.

Goering, Goebbels and Hitler – No Honour Among Thieves

'During a war, everybody loots a little bit. None of my so-called looting was illegal.'

Hermann Goering, 1946

Master of Europe

The look on their faces says it all. Goering is grinning from ear to ear, while beside him Hitler allows himself a smirk of satisfaction. It is the spring of 1940 and the pair have Europe at their feet, or rather on its knees. Hitler's strategic gamble has paid off handsomely. Against all expectations the Wehrmacht has outfoxed the French, Belgian and Dutch armies by staging an unexpected armoured assault through the narrow winding roads of the Ardennes, routing its historic enemies in just six weeks and leaving the shell-shocked British Expeditionary Force on the beaches of Dunkirk with their backs to the sea.

The victorious Germans cannot believe their luck. All doubts about the Austrian corporal's ability as a military leader have been dispelled and with them any chance the High Command might have had of toppling the dictatorship in a military coup. Hitler has achieved the impossible; reversing the humiliating defeat of 1918 and restoring Germany's pride, thereby fulfilling the role he believed Providence had bestowed upon him as saviour of the German people. The crowds who lined the streets of Berlin to hail their victorious Führer were euphoric, their gratitude mixed with relief, for many had feared a repeat of the stalemate of 1914–18.

But Hitler's military advisers are puzzled. Instead of finishing the British off in preparation for an invasion, Hitler orders his tanks to hold back, a fatal error which allows the British Expeditionary Force to stage a miraculous rescue of the remnants of their army so they can fight another day, although they have to abandon their heavy weapons and armoured vehicles in France.

None of this appears to trouble Hitler, who takes the opportunity for a brief sightseeing tour of Paris. As master of Europe he now has the key to the great treasure houses of France and Holland in his pocket. The vaults of the banks are open to him, the contents of private safe deposit boxes as well as government gold deposits are his for the asking, as are the precious contents of Europe's art galleries and museums. There are conspicuous gaps on their walls where once hung many a priceless masterpiece, for a number were spirited away in the last chaotic days of the Allied retreat. However, there were too many to hide. The German advance had been so swift it was all their curators and owners could do to save themselves.

In one gallery Hitler poses for a photo with Goering, the pair admiring *The Falconer* by Austrian master Hans Makart, held up for their appraisal by two uniformed SS men. The caption in the German papers will read: 'The Führer presents Reichsmarschall Goering with a gift in appreciation of his role in our historic victory.' The Führer is very generous. But then he does not have to pay for the presents he gives.

In due course the Führer's gift will be recorded in a 200-page close-lined ledger, showing the painting's title and the name of the artist, together with a brief description, the date it was acquired, its destination and the name of the collection or previous owner. The deprived owners were some of the most prominent art collectors and dealers in Europe, among them Rothschild, Rosenberg and Wildenstein, for private collections too were now part of the spoils of war. Vengeance played its part in Hitler's victory as did the opportunity to order the seizure of any painting, sculpture, tapestry or object belonging to the wealthy Jewish collectors he so despised.

Each entry in the Goering catalogue would be the envy of any art collector. *Venus* by Jacopo de Barbari, bought in Rome in April 1933 for the nominal sum of 12,000 lire, being one example. The following entries record similar trifling amounts and constitute the Hermann Goering collection, one of the largest private collections of priceless art in the world. But it would pale in comparison with the hoard acquired for the proposed Führermuseum in Linz.

GOERING'S ART COLLECTION BOASTED 250 SCULPTURES AND 168 TAPESTRIES WITH MANY NUDES AMONG HIS 2,000 LOOTED PAINTINGS

Altogether, the stolen art represented the largest case of organized theft in history, its value in 1945 being in excess of £160 million ($200m).

Goering's 'Passion' for Art

Details of this criminal undertaking would never have become public knowledge had it not been for Rose Valland, unofficial curator of the Jeu de Paume museum in Paris during the occupation. It was she who kept a secret record of Goering's periodic visits to the museum (some 20 in all) so that the priceless paintings could later be traced and hopefully returned to the museum, or their rightful owners.

It was due to her courage that the French Resistance was informed about the last of the trains carrying the looted art from Paris to Berlin and was able to intercept it. After the war she scoured eastern Europe tracking down the stolen paintings and it was during her personal treasure hunt that she chanced upon Goering's personal ledger detailing the 20 plus visits he had made to the Jeu de Paume looking for new acquisitions to complement his collection.

Goering would admit to having a 'passion' for collecting art while on trial for his life in Nuremberg in 1946 and to making a special effort to acquire the French Impressionists for his second wife, Emmy. He was the man who had everything and if he didn't own something he only had to ask and it would be delivered. However, even Goering did not dare to cream off pieces from the stack set aside for the Führermuseum, which was said to have comprised 5,000 works of art. But once the prize items had been allocated to Linz, it was every man for himself.

Goering had no particular liking for abstract and surrealist masters, but it galled him to think that paintings by Dali and Picasso would be destroyed by zealous Party functionaries simply because they had met with the Führer's disapproval. Especially as he could have sold them on to other members of the regime who had no problem with owning 'degenerate art' and who would then be in his debt.

The Reichsmarschall may have acquired an enviable collection, but he wasn't a discerning collector. Among the paintings he sold or exchanged for inferior works were Van Gogh's *Portrait of Doctor Gachet*, which was auctioned in Tokyo in 1990 for a record $82.5 million, and two priceless masters by Matisse (*Still Life With Sleeping Woman* and *Pianist and Checker Players*), which he swapped for an unremarkable nude by a minor 17th-century Dutch painter, Jan van Neck.

Though Goering expressed no interest in 'degenerate art', it appears that he had a distinct preference for nudes. Nancy Yeide, head of curatorial records at Washington's National Gallery of Art, spent seven years documenting Goering's collection, which boasted 250 sculptures and 168 tapestries, and discovered that there was 'a disproportionate number of nudes' among the 2,000 looted paintings.

Degenerate Art Exhibition

Goering is commonly associated with Nazi art theft on a grand scale, but his bitter rival Goebbels was also complicit in the questionable acquisition of priceless works of art.

In 1937 the Minister of Public Enlightenment and Propaganda – a title that Goebbels loathed – organized an exhibition of so-called *'Entartete Kunst'* ('degenerate art') comprising paintings, prints and sculptures that had been removed from public galleries because they were considered un-German and offensive to Aryan sensibilities. It was staged as a lurid sideshow to the main event, the Great German Art Exhibition, which had been mounted to celebrate the opening of the House of German Art on Prinzregentenstrasse, a short walk from Hitler's official private residence.

It was common knowledge that Hitler had an aversion to modern art in all its forms, which had been fermenting ever since he had been refused entry to the Viennese Academy of Fine Arts in 1907. The 17-year-old amateur artist had blamed his rejection on the Jewish members of the examination board, who had suggested that he might prefer to study architecture, though without a high school diploma Hitler knew he could not apply for a place on the course.

His watercolour sketches of Vienna's landmarks were crude and sold poorly, forcing him to go hungry and sleep rough until he came into a small inheritance from an aunt. But the stifling of his artistic ambitions had left him embittered and looking for someone to blame. His resentment was further inflamed after he read *Entartung* ('Degeneration'), a critique of turn of the century art and literature. The author, Max Nordau, a Hungarian Jew, had interpreted abstraction in modern art (specifically the work of the Symbolists but also the 'decadent' literature written by authors such as Wilde, Ibsen and Zola), as characteristic of diseased minds. He equated its rejection of realism, or classic representationalism, with an alarming decline in morality which in turn, he argued, had given rise to anti-Semitism. This latter point appears to have eluded Hitler, who was persuaded by Nordau's arguments to damn everything from Impressionism to Expressionism as symptomatic of a Jewish–Bolshevik conspiracy that had been conceived to corrupt Western civilization.

Goebbels knew that the Führer would take a personal interest in the galleries of National Socialist-approved painting and sculpture, which idealized the human form and extolled the simple virtues and pleasures of rural life or offered scenes of heroic self-sacrifice and comradeship under fire. He also hoped to ingratiate himself with the Führer by pandering to his violent dislike of modern art, so he insisted that each exhibit in the 'degenerate art' exhibition be labelled with contemptuous comments to ensure that it prompted the required horrified reaction from the public.

He also saw a chance to pocket a tidy sum by drawing crowds of art lovers and the merely curious, who would willingly pay to gawp and snigger at the most provocative examples of Dadaism, Futurism and Cubism. A publicity handout explained that the items on show were 'the poisonous flower of a Jewish parasitical plant grown on German soil', adding ominously, 'these will be the strongest proof for the necessity of a radical solution to the Jewish question'.

However, even the normally astute Goebbels was taken aback by the popularity of the 'forbidden' art exhibition, which attracted 2 million visitors in stark contrast to the 500,000 who paid to see the neoclassical sculptures by official Nazi artists Arno Breker and Josef Thorak and the kitsch chocolate box paintings by Adolf Wissel and Ludwig Dettmann.

To save face, the regime was forced to buy the unsold Breker and Thorak sculptures as well as Wissel and Dettmann's work. It was a humiliation for which Goebbels was blamed, but from which he swiftly recovered by suggesting that confiscated degenerate art could be quietly disposed of by being sold to private collectors abroad. The proceeds would be used to fund rearmament or to acquire 'old masters' for the proposed Führermuseum that Hitler planned for Linz.

Art Dealer to Goebbels

Once his scheme had been approved, Goebbels convened the Commission for the Exploitation of Degenerate Art, a four-man committee presided over by Hildebrand Gurlitt, a former museum curator and art expert with known Jewish ancestry but valuable connections to art dealers, collectors and museums abroad. Hildebrand is believed to have acquired over 300 priceless works of art for his own private collection at a nominal fee, purchasing them with foreign currency in accordance with Goebbels' instructions. It has been argued that some of the paintings were not so highly valued at the time, but the pitiably low price paid by Gurlitt and other Nazi-authorized dealers for such works would never have been accepted if the owner's life and liberty had not been at stake.

After the Fall of France in 1940, Gurlitt made frequent visits to Paris to acquire art from Jews who were desperate to leave before the next Nazi round-up. Some of them believed that they were entrusting a fellow Jew with their family heirlooms until they could be reunited with them after the war. It is alleged that Gurlitt also did the rounds of the capital's auction houses, picking up highly valuable pieces in so-called 'distress sales' which offered art that the owners felt compelled to sell in order to pay for their passage abroad. It was the time of the Reich Flight Tax and the Jewish Wealth Levy, both insidious Nazi schemes geared to fleece prosperous Jews of their savings.

Then in 1943, having proved his value to the Reich, he was personally entrusted with the acquisition of art for the proposed Führermuseum. On each transaction Gurlitt received a 5 per cent commission, which soon made him a very wealthy man. It was said that he used his authority to enter the abandoned homes of Jewish émigrés and remove whatever took his fancy. It has also been alleged that he ordered the opening of a bank vault in Bordeaux from which he took a Matisse masterpiece, *Seated Woman* (painted in 1921), belonging to the painter's friend Paul Rosenberg, who had fled to America. It is thought to be the single most valuable painting Gurlitt procured for his private collection, with an estimated value of between £5m–£6.5m ($6.4m–$8.3m).

Gurlitt later claimed that he had only agreed to be Goebbels' art dealer because it meant he would be spared a one-way ticket to Dachau. However, having a Jewish grandmother and therefore qualifying as a second-degree *Mischling* (person of mixed race) was not an automatic qualification for the transports. He might even have believed that by buying art he was giving the persecuted a chance to evade capture, but the fact remains that he was accumulating a vast private collection of art for a fraction of its true value. This included pieces by Chagall, Matisse, Picasso, Dürer, Delacroix, Renoir and Canaletto: a collection which would eventually comprise over 1,200 paintings, prints and etchings, valued after the war at more than £800 million ($1,000m).

Substantial though the Gurlitt hoard was, it was only the tip of the mountain of looted treasures that the Nazis plundered during their 12-year reign of terror. It is believed that 650,000 separate works of art including paintings, prints, sculptures, tapestries, books, antique furniture and miscellaneous *objets d'art* were stolen by the Nazis, the majority of which remain unclaimed by their rightful owners or their heirs.

A Divided France

Following the signing of the surrender in the very same train in which the Germans had signed the armistice of 1918, the Nazi administration divided France into an occupied and an unoccupied zone. The *zone occupée in* the north contained the greater part of the country's industry, the majority of the population and the best, or *grand cru*, vineyards. The remainder was left to a puppet administration under the elderly Marshal Pétain, which was commonly and contemptuously referred to as the Vichy regime, implying that Pétain and his ministers were no better than collaborators. The French people's respect for the hero of Verdun was soon offset by the anger generated by Vichy's adoption of Nazi policies under which Jews were stripped of their citizenship, trade unions were abolished, communists and Freemasons were imprisoned and women were prohibited from the professions. The Republic's cherished values of 'Liberty, Equality, Fraternity' were abandoned for the insidious maxim of '*Travail, Famille, Patrie*' ('Work, Family, Fatherland'), echoing the Nazis' slogan '*Kinder, Küche, Kirche*' ('Children, Kitchen, Church').

In Alsace, French was outlawed and its inhabitants were threatened with deportation if they dared to speak their own language. Every outward sign of the region's historic links with France was erased. Even the street signs were changed for their German equivalent and the regions' winegrowers found they were now restricted to selling to Germans at prices the occupation forces determined were 'fair and reasonable'.

More distressing to the local inhabitants was the directive ordering their children to join the Hitler Youth and the conscription of all young men into the German army.

The division of France was a shrewd and cynical move on behalf of the Nazis, who were at once relieved of the responsibility and the manpower required to administer an area amounting to two-fifths of the country, which had been flooded with an estimated 10 million refugees fleeing from their homes in the north. It also gave the Germans a free hand to plunder the resources and treasures of the occupied zone.

Wine

'The real profiteers of this war are ourselves and out of it we shall come bursting with fat! We shall give back nothing and will take everything we can make use of.'

Adolf Hitler

Hitler did not drink wine – in fact the one time he sampled vintage French wine he dismissed it as 'vulgar vinegar' – but he saw no reason why that should prevent him from hoarding half a million bottles of some of the finest French champagne, cognac and port in a cave above the Eagle's Nest at Berchtesgaden.

(This was the name given to the structure high above the Berghof, the Führer's summer residence. It was designed by Bormann as a present for Hitler's 50th birthday though he rarely used it.) Vintage wine, after all, was as precious as any other commodity in short supply. It was as desirable as a priceless work of art and an investment in uncertain times.

Rare wines commanded high prices and here, at the foot of the Alps, secure behind thick steel doors, were inestimable riches – the wealth of the most eminent vineyards in Bordeaux, Burgundy and Vouvray in the Loire valley. Chateau Latour, Chateau Lafite-Rothschild, Chateau Mouton Rothschild, Romanée-Conti and Chateau d'Yquem. Labels to delight the palette of the oenophile, or discerning wine-lover.

It was a staggering sight – crate upon crate stacked to the roof and extending far back into the shadows. The former owners would have been horrified to see how their precious produce was being stored, but they knew that they were lucky to have lost only their merchandise. Although 1940 might not have been a vintage year for French wine, it had been a good year for German wine connoisseurs. They could take what they liked from the best-stocked cellars in northern France and did not have to pay a pfennig for it. They didn't even incur the cost of transporting it back to Germany. French trains were commandeered to carry it across the border, driven by French drivers and engineers at the point of a loaded gun.

But the French winemakers had lost more than just merchandise. The wholesale ransacking of their cellars and the occupation of their vineyards by the hated 'Boche' was a humiliating loss of national identity and pride. Winemaking was a sacred art entrusted to those who had learned its alchemical secrets. In acknowledgement of this, the French government accorded the winegrowers the distinction of delaying their conscription until the harvest was in and had sent military labour detachments to the vineyards to help with the harvest.

Hiding the Bottles

They needn't have bothered. That year the crop was uncommonly poor. Bad weather was to blame, but the peasants had seen it coming. They had a saying in that part of France. A poor harvest signifies the coming of war. While the war dragged on the quality of the grapes would be mediocre and only at its end would there be a fine crop. The Germans would be welcome to the bitter wartime harvest. But their stocks of vintage wine were another matter. They were a family heirloom and must be safeguarded at all costs. In fact, they were more than that. They were a symbol of French national pride, or as former prime minister Edouard Daladier described it: 'France's most precious jewel.'

THANKS TO THE BREATHING SPACE, FRENCH WINEGROWERS WERE ABLE TO HIDE THEIR MOST PRECIOUS STOCK IN INGENIOUS WAYS

Thanks to the breathing space offered by the so-called 'phoney war' – the eight months of eerie calm that followed the declaration of war on 3 September 1939 – resourceful French winegrowers were able to hide some of their most precious stock in ingenious ways.

Men such as Maurice Drouhin stored tens of thousands of bottles in caves under Beaune, the wine capital of Burgundy in the Côte d'Or. The maze of caves offered plenty of natural hiding places. In one Maurice built a false wall to secure his stock of vintage Romanée-Conti while his wife and children collected spiders to place at its foot, where they would hopefully spin their webs to disguise the new bricks and fresh cement.

Elsewhere other wine producers were utilizing their underground stores to hide weapons and any possessions they didn't want the invaders to seize. The scale of the operation can be gleaned from the fact that one of the smaller champagne producers sought to hide sufficient stock to fill 100,000 bottles, a fraction of what the larger houses attempted to conceal in the labyrinth of limestone caves that honeycombed the region.

It wasn't only the winegrowers who were stung into a panic to protect their valuable wine stores that May. Restaurant owner André Terrail had spent a lifetime accumulating one of the finest cellars in Paris and was not prepared to see it fall into the hands of 'the old enemy'. His restaurant, La Tour d'Argent on the quai de la Tournelle, was renowned for its cuisine and for its 400-page wine list, which boasted bottles dating back to the time of Napoleon. It drew film stars such as Charlie Chaplin and Marlene Dietrich, while writers such as Ernest Hemingway and Marcel Proust had celebrated its dishes and distinctive atmosphere in print.

When news of the German breakthrough reached André's son Claude in Lyon, he took emergency leave from the air force to try and save the most valuable bottles, saying that to be a Frenchman meant to fight for both your country and its wine. He and his small staff managed to wall in 20,000 bottles before the Wehrmacht marched in to find the capital almost deserted.

Within hours an emissary from Goering's Air Ministry arrived and demanded to be shown the famous cellars, especially the bottles from 1867. He was informed that they had all been drunk and was taken down to the cellars to see for himself. After a fruitless two-hour search, the German had no choice but to admit defeat. He did not leave empty-handed however, because he ordered the seizure of the remaining 80,000 bottles. The same strategy was adopted throughout northern France by hoteliers and restaurateurs, who were determined that the Germans should not be allowed to get their hands on their finest wines.

Champagne Looting Spree

The first step for the Wehrmacht occupying Bordeaux was to billet its troops in the region's numerous chateaux. The owners were ordered to leave immediately and were allowed to take only what they could carry with them. Some had the foresight to move their valuables and antiques into the attic, while others were told to leave and take their furniture with them.

The Miaihles family carried their Charles X furniture and collection of early-19th-century art to the attic then dragged a heavy armoire in front of a door leading down to the wine cellar. However, the Germans who occupied the chateau were no fools. They soon discovered the hidden door and the cellar. Their commanding officer reproved the family for trying to deceive them, but he seemed more offended by the fact that they evidently believed he and his men would have ransacked the place like barbarians.

'Do you think we are thieves?' he asked them.

Had he known that the family were sheltering their Jewish friends at another chateau he would certainly not have allowed them to leave alive.

However, the family were uncommonly fortunate. The

officer kept his word and none of the wine belonging to the Miaihles was touched. Not all the Germans were so considerate. Through June and July they looted with impunity and drank bottles of vintage champagne as carelessly as if it was cheap table wine.

In the village of Mesnil-sur-Oger a convoy of 15 vehicles pulled up in front of the Delamotte champagne house. A young German officer stepped out from the leading vehicle and announced that Field Marshal Goering had ordered him to confiscate their stocks of champagne. Over the course of the next few days, hundreds of cases were carried from the cellars of the most prestigious champagne houses. In total an estimated 2 million bottles were taken from the region that had given its name to that sparkling wine, along with anything else that took the invaders' fancy. Food and clothing and cases of expensive wine were piled high in the village squares, while the inhabitants looked on helplessly. Seventeen-year-old Bernard de Nonancourt worked for Delamotte and recalled that the men who worked for Goering were more 'brutal' and 'played the black market'.

The Fat Man made absolutely no apologies for the behaviour of his men.

'I intend to plunder,' he told the Occupation Authority, 'and plunder copiously.'

Goering shamelessly and brazenly stole to stock his own cellars, which boasted one of the finest collections of rare and vintage wines in the Reich. The Reichsmarschall considered victory over the French had given him the right to procure their best bottles for his own use. He took a special pleasure in opening a bottle of Lafite-Rothschild late at night and would then become uncommonly sociable. Albert Speer had always found Goering to be gruff and unapproachable, but remembered that the one time he found him agreeable was when they shared a bottle of Lafite-Rothschild. Goering's fondness for vintage champagne and Hitler's aversion to any alcohol may have been the reason why the Reichsmarschall kept his social visits to the Berghof to a minimum.

Hitler was notorious for his interminable monologues, which consisted of rambling reminiscences and monotonous lectures which his regular guests knew by heart. In order to stay awake into the early hours and disguise their lack of interest, they would drink sparkling wine and champagne, only it was invariably second-rate as Goering had appropriated the best bottles for himself.

Once the looting spree was over and commercial relations with the population were put on a more regular footing, Goering exercised his powers as ruler of economic policy for the occupied countries by devaluing the franc, so that German soldiers could buy more for their marks. Whatever they didn't take by force they could now buy for a fraction of its true value. French perfume, fashion and cosmetics were sent home by the crateload and copious amounts of expensive champagne and cognac were consumed by euphoric troops savouring the rewards of a swift and unexpected victory.

But dividing the spoils of war exposed the divisions within the Nazi leadership. Goering saw France as no more than a subjugated municipality of the Reich and wanted to bleed it dry, whereas Foreign Minister and former champagne salesman von Ribbentrop argued that it would be in Germany's interest to allow France a degree of sovereignty. In the latter case, the French might be persuaded that collaboration could be in their best interest.

Nazi Wine Traders

In order to foster a working relationship with the French the looting had to stop and the wine had to be paid for. However, Goering knew that the common soldier could not be expected to distinguish a Burgundy from a Bordeaux, and so he established a special unit of experienced wine connoisseurs conscripted from the German wine trade. These German weinführers, as the locals called them, were told to make the French producers a not too generous offer so that the wine could be resold at a huge profit, aided by the devalued franc. Unfortunately for Goering, the men he entrusted with this task were old friends of the major French wine producers and had learned their trade in the very same vineyards and champagne houses that they were now being ordered to deceive. Men such as Otto Klaebisch, Adolphe Segnitz and Heinz Bomers had been doing business with the French champagne houses long before Hitler came to power and expected to do so after the war was over. There was a mutual respect that even National Socialist zeal could not destroy.

Bomers' father had been a senator in the Bremen administration in 1930 when Goering was the prime minister of Middle Saxony and at the time he had refused to meet Goering, who was notorious for his unforgiving nature. Bomers' son Heinz accepted the commission to go to France only after certain conditions were accepted, one being that he would not be paid and another that he was given the authority to intervene if he saw the occupying troops acting brutally.

But not all of Bordeaux's inhabitants welcomed him back. Some resented the power that he now exercised over them and observed that they had little choice but to sell to the Germans as the British and American markets were not open to them any longer. Either that or they could dump their produce in the river, as one disgruntled producer recalled. However, one wine producer had little to complain about when Bomers offered to relieve him of large quantities of substandard stock which he knew his German customers wouldn't know from the finest French wines. On another occasion, Bomers saved several cases of Chateau Mouton Rothschild by advising the French producer to glue the prestigious label to bottles of *vin ordinaire* and ship those off to Berlin instead.

Ironically, the Germans did not profit from their monopoly of the French wine market because the harvests of 1939–41 were particularly poor. The weather was largely to blame, but even if the yield had been good there would not have been the manpower to harvest much of it as the young able-bodied Frenchmen had been interned with the rest of the vanquished army. Unripened grapes could still be used if sugar was added to boost the alcohol content, but the war had brought a sugar shortage. Nor could the wine be clarified to remove the particles that cloud it as this was traditionally done using egg white which was as scarce as sugar.

Much of the wine of 1940, the year of Hitler's blitzkrieg, was so poor the French producers poured it on to the ground. It seemed as if there was something in the old adage after all. When the Germans were driven out in 1944 and France had been liberated, the vineyards produced a bountiful crop. It was both a good year for France and for French wine.

'It was Hitler's regime, Hitler's policy, Hitler's rule of force, Hitler's victory and Hitler's defeat – nothing else.'
Hans Frank at Nuremberg, 1946

Resources

Hitler's Women Channel 4 (2001)

Górecki, Henryk *The Symphony of Sorrowful Songs* (Voiceprint 2007)

Norton, Rictor (ed.) *'One day they were simply gone': The Nazi Persecution of Homosexuals,* 21 December 1999, updated 10 August 2010 http://rictornorton.co.uk/nazi.htm

The Spectator 23 February 1940

www.alphahistory.com

www.en.wikipedia.org

www.fold3.com

www.history.ac.uk

www.jewishvirtuallibrary.org

www.nizkor.org

www.spartacus.schoolnet.co.uk

www.spiegel.de

www.usmbooks.com

Bibliography

Delarue, Jacques *Trafic et Crimes sous l'Occupation* (Fayard 1993)

Evans, Richard *The Third Reich in Power* (Penguin 2006)

Fest, Joachim *Hitler* (Vintage Books 1975)

Fromm, Bella *Blood and Banquets* (Citadel Press 1998)

Heiden, Konrad *The Fuehrer* (Robinson 1999)

Heston, Renate and Heston, Leonard *The Medical Casebook of Adolf Hitler* (Harper Collins .1979)

Hitler, Adolf *Mein Kampf* (Munich 2016)

Igra, Samuel *Germany's National Vice* (publisher unknown 1945)

Katcher, Lisolette (nurse) *Hitler's Women* (Channel 4)

Kladstrup, Donald and Kladstrup, Petie *Wine and War* (Hodder 2002)

Knopp, Guido *Hitler's Henchmen* (Sutton Publishing 2000)

Knopp, Guido *Hitler's Women* (History Press 2006)

Kruger, Horst *A Crack in the Wall* (Fromm International 1986)

Kubizek, August *The Young Hitler I Knew* (Greenhill Books 2006)

Langer, Walter *The Mind of Adolf Hitler* (Pan Macmillan 1974)

Lively, Scott *The militant homosexual core of the National Socialist Party* (Leadership University 1996)

Luthy, Herbert 'Der Führer Persönlich' (*Der Monat*, No. 62, 1953)

Moorhouse, Roger *Berlin at War* (Vintage 2011)

Morgan, Patrick *Hitler's Henchmen* (Demand 2014)

Petropoulos, Jonathan *Art as Politics in the Third Reich* (University of North Carolina Press 1999)

Rauschning, Hermann *Germany's Revolution of Destruction* (Heinemann 1939)

Rector, Frank *The Nazi Extermination of Homosexuals* (Stein and Day 1981)

Rees, Laurence *Auschwitz* (BBC Books 2005)

Rigg, Bryan *Hitler's Jewish Soldiers* (University Press of Kansas 2002)

Roland, Paul *History of the Nazis* (Arcturus/Capella 2009)

Roland, Paul *The Nazi Files* (Arcturus 2014)

Seward, Desmond *Napoleon and Hitler* (Viking Press 1989)

Shirer, William *The Rise and Fall of the Third Reich* (Arrow 1991)

Snyder, Louis *Encyclopedia of the Third Reich* (Paragon House 1989)

Snyder, Louis *Hitler's Henchmen* (David and Charles 2005)

Speer, Albert *Inside the Third Reich* (Weidenfeld & Nicolson 2009)

Strasser, Otto *The Gangsters Around Hitler* (W. H. Allen 1942)

Taber, George *Chasing Gold* (Pegasus 2014)

Taylor, Fred *The Goebbels Diaries: 1939–1941* (G. P. Putmans 1983)

Van Capelle, Henk *Hitler's Henchmen* (Gallery Books 1990)

Waite, Robert G. *The Psychopathic God: Adolf Hitler* (Signet Books 1977)

Wachsmann, Nikolaus *KL: A History of the Nazi Concentration Camps* (Abacus 2016)

Wright, Gordon *The Ordeal of Total War* (Waveland PR Inc. 1997)

Index